GRACIOUSLY KEEP ME THIS NIGHT

DEVOTIONS FROM SCRIPTURE'S DARKEST HOURS

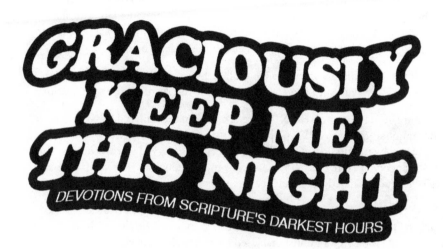

GRACIOUSLY KEEP ME THIS NIGHT

DEVOTIONS FROM SCRIPTURE'S DARKEST HOURS

Steve Kruschel

Foreword by Michael Berg

Published by:
1517 Publishing
PO Box 54032
Irvine, CA 92619-4032

Publisher's Cataloging-In-Publication Data
(Prepared by The Donohue Group, Inc.)

Names: Kruschel, Steve, author. | Berg, Mike, 1978- writer of supplementary textual content.
Title: Graciously keep me this night : devotions from scripture's darkest hours / by Steve Kruschel ; foreword by Michael Berg.
Description: Irvine, CA : 1517 Publishing, [2022] | Includes bibliographical references.
Identifiers: ISBN 9781948969277 (paperback) | ISBN 9781948969970 (ebook)
Subjects: LCSH: Consolation—Religious aspects—Christianity—Prayers and devotions. | Hope—Religious aspects—Christianity—Prayers and devotions. | Word of God (Christian theology)—Prayers and devotions. | LCGFT: Devotional literature.
Classification: LCC BV4905.3 .K78 2022 (print) | LCC BV4905.3 (ebook) | DDC 248.86—dc23

Printed in the United States of America.

Cover art by Zachariah James Stuef.

To my lovely wife, Becca,
because I forgot to dedicate my first book to her.

Contents

Foreword

Michael Berg

Pastor Steven Kruschel carries on the great Lutheran tradition of producing pastoral devotional material for God's people. In his first devotional, *The Pastoral Prophet: Meditations on the Book of Jeremiah*, Rev. Kruschel made alive the story of Jeremiah, "The Weeping Prophet", by applying the story of the prophet's weakness and God's strength to our own day. Kruschel has now delivered this meditation, *Graciously Keep Me this Night: Devotions from Scripture's Darkest Hours*, as a gift to all who suffer through long nights of apprehension and doubt.

Devotional material was in hot demand in sixteenth-century Germany. Frederick the Wise even commissioned Luther to write devotionals and sermons for his own personal use. This thirst for quality gospel preaching and written devotional material demanded to be quenched, and the early reformers rose to the challenge. The reformers' written devotionals are historically underappreciated. What the early reformers did for hymnody they also did for personal devotions. By sermon, hymn, and devotion, the gospel's bright light began to shine again on those living in the darkness of works-righteous law. Pastor Kruschel has dedicated his writing skills to continuing this honorable tradition.

We too thirst for this same gospel as did those five hundred years ago. It's the same devil, the same urge to earn God's favor, the same temptations of the flesh only in a contemporary garb. And it is the same gospel of Christ, confessed by the apostles, mused upon by the fathers, and preached by the reformers that we hold onto to so dearly.

The gospel is often obscured when the church turns only to academic endeavors. God's people need to hear again the freshness of the gospel in their *vernacular*, not only their own language but also in their own context. They need a preacher. How else would they hear the gospel (Rom. 10:14)? So we preach. We preach not to just to brains but to souls. We preach to real people. And real people have real problems. They harbor real anger. They are haunted by real doubts. They suffer real depression. They agonize over real problems. They endure long nights.

A happy god will not do. A happy god only offers empty platitudes and invites us to think positively. Too often the American god is just that, a happy God. Sure, he might get angry at our enemies, those people who are not like us, but he is pleased with us and blesses us. This is how we know that God loves us, by the blessings we enjoy. But what about the afflicted soul? The last thing a cancer patient needs is another trite cliché. The last thing the parent of a mentally ill son needs is another speech on the goodness of God. What they need is a God who suffers with them and for them. They need the gospel.

You are not alone as you endure long nights. We know this because of the promises of God. We also know this because he was with his people in the past. These are the stories the Holy Spirit puts before our weary eyes in Scripture. Pastor Kruschel uses these inspired stories of afflicted souls to speak to you, his reader. He begins with the darkness of the early verses of Genesis and makes his way through God's Word all the way to the "obliteration" of darkness in Revelation 22. You will hear about Samson, Ruth, and David. You will relate to Mary, Peter, and Paul. You will see saints who are weak but strong in Christ. You will see yourself as the same, a saint in the blood of Christ who is afflicted by this world's temptations but made whole in Christ.

This is the real God. A real, gritty, and personal God. One not unsympathetic without sufferings but one who endured it all in our place without sin (Heb. 4:15). This is the gospel: that Christ lived the perfect life to replace your imperfect life and died the perfect death to pay the price for your sins. So that no matter what dark moment you are in now or will find yourself in the future, you have an eternal hope. God does not encourage us to run away from the darkness, but rather he grants us permission to enter the darkness. In baptism he brings us into his death at the cross (Rom. 6) and raises us to a new life now and forever. So if we have already died and risen with him, what darkness could overwhelm us now? You are never alone during your dark nights. You have a God who is always there with this gospel message, "My grace is sufficient for you" (2 Cor. 12:9).

Introduction

I've been told that to die in your dreams is to perish in real life. But what does it mean when death wakes up with you? I still remember the night death woke up with me. It hung in my room and I couldn't move to stop it. I couldn't run to escape it.

My own paralyzed body imprisoned me.

Sleep paralysis is a scientific term for this ancient, nightmarish problem. If you suffer from it, you know just how horrifying it can be. The effects sound like the stuff of science fiction—but I assure you it remains all too real. Sleep paralysis catches you between your dream world and the real world. It wakes up your mind before your body can move. That is when the real-life nightmares arrive.

Some who struggle with sleep paralysis swear they have seen dark figures enter their room. Others felt the hands of demons slowly wrap around their ankles, pulling them down through their bed. And some have even experienced a severe pushing down on their chest, feeling as though they are going to asphyxiate in their sleep.

I know how they feel. I also suffer from sleep paralysis. The experience is more terrifying than the scariest horror film, as though some insidious force hit pause and pulled me into the movie. I thought I was going to die. I was in high school at the time, sleeping in the black recesses of the basement. I had woken up in the middle of the night, feeling the darkest of presences—as though the devil himself were standing over my bed.

I didn't move. I *couldn't* move. With my head on the pillow, the covers partially over my head I just wanted to go back into the blissful ignorance of sleep all over again. But I couldn't. My own sleeping arms and legs imprisoned my mind. I could still think. I was still awake. But try as I may, I could not think my way out of the frightening situation.

That's when my bed started to move—not the whole bed, just the corner by my feet. The mattress pushed down as though someone was sitting on the end. My mind raced. Had the devil himself just arrived? That's what it felt like. Had I unknowingly done something to invite him into my world? What could I possibly do now? I was powerless.

On and on the night went. My heart was racing. Hours seemed to pass as this evil presence sat on the edge of my bed.

That's when I started to pray. I couldn't speak the words. I still couldn't move at all. I pleaded with the Lord in my mind. The thoughts all blurred together the way they do when fear floods the soul.

And God answered my prayers. My longest night—a harrowing experience I'll never forget—finally ended. The sun came up. My bed became still. I could *move* again. I just never wanted to sleep again. I wanted to hold insomnia like a shield against whatever might appear with the following night.

In the years since that long evening, I have been told that I experienced sleep paralysis. Countless others have encountered similar situations: the inability to move, feeling an evil presence entering the room, an overwhelming fright from deep within themselves. The devil may not have been in my room that night—he could have been, I'm still not sure—but that experience still frightens me to the point where he might as well have been there.

That was my longest night. What caused yours?

Maybe my nighttime recollections sound all too familiar to you. If so, my heart goes out to you. I wouldn't wish that night on my worst enemy. But maybe the entire story sounds foreign. I understand that, too. Other people's long nights can sound strange to me also. That's where God's Word steps in, bringing me into the harsh realities of other people's long nights to witness the suffering…and to hear his timeless comfort.

But something caused your longest night. What was it?

Have you kept watch over the bed of your dying child, unwilling to fall asleep? "Powerless" doesn't begin to describe just how weak and ineffective you feel. Minute after minute you pray to God that you could take her place in an exchange that would enable her to grow up and live a full life. And really, you won't be able to live much after she's gone anyway.

Maybe your long night turned you inward. You were betrayed by your closest friend, or shunned by a family that no longer wants anything to do with you. The black hours of depression finally drag you to the question that you dare not vocalize: Should I just end my life? Would anyone even care if I was gone?

Spiritual turmoil can stop a peaceful night in its tracks too. The devil delights in sliding doubts into our lonely minds in the evening. Temptations take cover under darkness.

Maybe you have another struggle that casts insomnia on you—something far worse than what I've listed. Whatever it is, I ask that you please read on. This book is not in your hands so that we can simply commiserate with each other's difficulties. It is meant to pierce your sin-darkened night with the light of God's Word. These devotions promise to show you just how strong and eternal and loving your Light is. These words rest in front of you to show you Jesus.

Can I tell you about a particularly long night Jesus once had? It probably isn't the night you are thinking of. It took place at the beginning of the most important week in history: Holy Week. It remains one of my favorite moments in Jesus' ministry, and only one of the gospels mentions it.

"Jesus went into the temple courts in Jerusalem and looked around at everything. Since it was already late, he went out to Bethany with the Twelve" (Mark 11:11). This probably wasn't the longest night of Jesus' ministry, but it seems to be the most interesting. After Jesus rode into Jerusalem on Palm Sunday, after the roaring of the crowds subsided and the cries of "Hosanna" stopped echoing off the walls of the ancient city...Jesus stuck around.

Jesus *looked* around.

What was he looking at? What was he thinking about? The temple stood in front of him, perhaps taking him back to King David's building of the altar and Solomon's construction of the building. He could recollect the destruction of that first temple and the rebuilding of the second one.

Did he look around at the city of Jerusalem, thinking back on all the prophets who were killed within her walls? As the Lamb of God, did he see the smoke of the past slowly rising up from the altar of a million burning sacrifices? Or was he simply looking at his church for the last time, the way we longingly watch our church as we drive away?

It is here at this paused moment in time, dear reader, that Jesus meets you. Call it the calm before the storm, or the deep blackness of despair or the longest night of your life—ultimately your deepest fears are your Savior's greatest opportunity to show his love in your life.

I write these devotions as one who has somberly sat out the night. I know you have your own awful memories too. That is why I ask you to read on. Each of these devotions marks a moment in Scripture when someone faced a long night. The woman who felt the cut of betrayal slice into her heart. The disciple who struggled through the doubt. The parents who powerlessly watched over their dying child. These individuals were many things, but none of them were ever alone.

You are not alone either. Jesus cannot remind you of that truth enough. To hammer that point home, Jesus uses one phrase so often in his word that it might have lost its meaning in your life. But the phrase means everything: "Don't be afraid."

In the midst of the most frightening moments in the human experience, when ships were sinking and the sky was falling, while armies charged forward and the fires of persecutions burned their hottest, one phrase rang out from the Lord through his messengers. It remained a proclamation of peace in the most troubling times: "Don't be afraid."

The fear was usually palpable. Sometimes the circumstances caused it. Other times the very messenger of peace fueled the fear. On every occasion, the words needed to be proclaimed, like a great and mighty promise: "Don't be afraid."

Whether you are reading these devotions during the 40 dark days of Lent, or if blackness is apprehending you at a different time of year, let these three words of promise light your path. "Don't be afraid." The words themselves are timeless in their beauty, sophisticated in their simplicity, and powerful in their proclamation. Your Lord speaks these comforting words to you, too.

Struggling with doubt? Don't be afraid—your Savior's word will strengthen your faith. Flooding your bed with guilty tears every night? Don't be afraid—your Jesus took away all of your sins. Fearing the darkness and the enemies it hides? Don't be afraid—your protecting Lord has won your every victory.

And so, I would like to end this beginning with a prayer. The writer of this prayer was a man who experienced his own fair share of long nights. He wrote it with your nightmares in mind. The Lord who took your punishment and hell on a sin-darkened cross, promises to graciously keep you through this night, and every night. Now and always.

Martin Luther's Evening Prayer

I thank you my heavenly Father, through Jesus Christ your dear Son, that you have graciously kept me this day. Forgive me all my sins and graciously keep me this night. Into your hands I commend my body and soul and all things. Let your holy angel be with me that the wicked foe may have no power over me. Amen.

Chapter 1

Darkness Created

Genesis 1:1-5; John 1:1-5

"In the beginning, God created the heavens and the earth" (Gen 1:1). You probably know those words so well that they feel like coming home. But can you actually visualize what is happening? The picture has remained difficult to grasp even for the most gifted minds. What comes next remains even stranger. God describes an indescribable scene with a strange Hebrew phrase: *tohu vavohu*. The earth was "formless and empty" (Gen 1:2). For us creatures who are used to seeing the forms and shapes of creation, this picture is a difficult sight to imagine. Making matters worse is the darkness. In the beginning it covered everything.

And yet, while the darkened heavens and earth remained formless, the Spirit of God hovered over the waters. The powerful, triune God would form the formless. Father, Son and Holy Spirit would finish the unfinished. The trinity would cause light to pierce the darkness.

"Let there be light" (Gen 1:3). The first words we ever hear God speak shine light into existence. What a sight—light and darkness swirling around one another like oil and water! No star yet pulsated to give light an origin. No black hole existed yet to void that light from space. These two integral parts of creation simply stood next to each other amidst God's vast, formless heavens and earth. So, God simply divided them. "He separated the light from the darkness" (Gen 1:4).

How incomprehensible! Go ahead and meditate on these opening verses of the Bible. Take a week or a month and try to reckon the relationship of light and darkness in a sinless, formless creation. After months, or years, of careful, prayerful consideration you will probably end up at the same place the Apostle Paul did: "What fellowship does light have with darkness?" (2 Cor 6:14).

It is a good question. The two stand as opposites in every sense. Physically, light and darkness chase each other away, taking turns as the conqueror. Scientifically, light particles speed through space like waves. Spiritually, light shines forth knowledge and hope and perfection while darkness causes blindness and degradation and sinfulness. That's the way Paul was describing light and darkness for the Corinthians.

That type of perfect light filled God's sinless universe. That type of darkness was coming for God's perfect creation.

The formless, empty heavens and earth took shape one day at a time. Light and darkness, day and night, sea and sky, land and plants, stars and moon, fish and birds, animals and mankind all came about by God's perfect word in splendid order. "God saw everything that he had made, and indeed, it was very good" (Gen 1:31).

Even the darkness.

Thousands of years after God spoke everything into being, long after Adam and Eve fell into sin, God indicated to the prophet Isaiah that all of this creating prowess proved his divinity. "I am the one who forms light and creates darkness, the one who makes peace and creates disaster. I am the Lord, the one who does all these things" (Isa 45:7).

But why? Why create darkness at all? Is there ever a need for the sun to set? Certainly darkness can harmlessly fill the lightless voids of a perfect universe, but how disastrous the night has become in this sinful world! The Bible is filled with sinful actions that could only be accomplished under the cover of darkness. Loneliness and depression haunt sinful souls when the world becomes black.

Night after night, our devotions will sit us next to lost souls longing for light in the midst of darkness. Calm will lead to shouts. Stillness descends into chaos. Night will come, when darkness will seem to reign forever. And here we will sit in the middle of it.

The men and women of Scripture dreaded their own personal demons in the darkness. But what keeps you up at night? What guilt-ridden thoughts does the darkness place at the doorstep of your conscience? What sins or which betrayals make you wish that your triune God had never called the darkness into being? I have mine. Throughout the course of these devotions I will try to be brave enough to share some of them so you can see how much I appreciate your struggles. But you have to be honest about your struggles in the night, too.

Call back your mental picture of the formless and empty heavens and earth. I know, it is difficult to imagine, but try. You might see God the Father standing over everything, a great beard hanging between outstretched hands. Maybe you see the Holy Spirit hovering over the deep. But don't forget Jesus. He was there in the beginning, too.

He was the Word. He created the light and the darkness. He watched as the perfect couple, made in his image, descended into sin. He sat with their saddened descendants. He waited out the long nights with his tear-filled followers.

And then he accomplished a most amazing miracle. It is as difficult to understand as the formless heavens and the darkened earth. "The Word became flesh" (John 1:14). The Light of the world chose to live in the darkness of sin. But as the Light of the world, Jesus didn't let the darkness chase him away. He used it to mediate and pray to his Father. He saw the darkness, imperfect as it had become. And then he let that darkness of sin reign. The Word allowed himself to be captured. The Peace of the world said nothing to stop the war waged against him. The Light of the world allowed himself to be snuffed out on a cross of wood.

"What fellowship does light have with darkness?" (2 Cor 6:14).

There was no fellowship on the cross between the Lord of light and the darkness of sin and hell. This was no handshake. No communion could be had. Jesus took the punishment of hell for all of our dark deeds. The pain and the sorrow that accompanied it all led the Lord himself to speak out in the midst of darkness—a statement as important as "let there be light" (Gen 1:3). A declaration of victory. The creation of salvation. "It is finished" (John 19:30).

The sun stopped shining that day. Darkness chased away the light. The shouting crowds eventually quieted down. Everyone left the darkest scene the world had ever beheld.

It all made way for the brightest day of all.

Even darkness could not hold on to the Light of the world, the Resurrection and the Life. The Son of God rose again in victory over the blackness of death. He assured you of light and life and eternity with him in heaven.

He assures you of that sure and certain future even while you walk through this valley where death hangs over you as a shadow. You might be up tonight struggling with illness. Maybe sleep evades you because someone you love betrayed you. Perhaps guilt haunts your dreams.

You do not sit alone tonight. You never have. The Light of the world sits with you. He will never leave you, no matter how dark the night appears. He has conquered your every enemy: sin, death, the devil and even the darkness. Do not be afraid. Right now your risen Lord is preparing a place for you in his heaven. There is no darkness there. Sleep does not elude God's children within her walls. In fact, there is no night at all. No formlessness. No emptiness.

Just the Son…who shines on you forever.

Comfort for the Night

"Do not be afraid. I am the First and the Last—the Living One. I was dead and, see, I am alive forever and ever!" (Rev 1:17).

CHAPTER 2

Banished from Bliss

Genesis 3:15-24

The sins of fathers don't just cripple their children; they forever haunt the hearts of the fathers themselves. Fathers remember the day when their discipline perhaps went too far. They feel that lament in their heart every day. Each dad recalls his shortcomings as a breadwinner—the hard years when income was tight and he felt he had failed his family. And every father remembers the day when his mistake damaged his family. His loved ones may not have been ruined forever, but even one broken day feels like an eternity of disappointment.

To be sure, fathers have not cornered the market on grief and failure. Mothers feel failure, too. Children spend their lives attempting to overcome moments of grief and loss. But if God has taught us anything through our world's first family, it is that feelings of guilt with which we struggle all had their origin in the head of the household in the Garden of Eden. Adam had let his family down. As a husband he had failed his wife. As the future father of the world, he had ruined his children. Over and over again Scripture reminds us of the consequences of our father's fall: "For as in Adam they all die" (1 Cor 15:22).

On the evening after his fall into sin, Adam must have contended with an overwhelming amount of guilt. No doubt the events of the day turned over and over in his mind. How could he have let his own wife, Eve, listen to the devil? Why had he not intervened? Would this heavy shame ever become easier to bear?

If Adam's own feelings of failure and loss smoldered in his heart, a glance over to his wife, Eve, would have caused his heart to completely burn out. It is hard enough to bear the grief for your own sinful consequences. It can be unbearable to watch your failures hurt your own family—the woman you love—the beloved wife that God has given to you.

Did Adam get any sleep that first night after he had fallen into sin? How could he? The effects of his sin were inescapable. A midnight walk through the fields would reveal thorns and thistles—a curse from his sin. A glance back to the Garden would cause his eyes to squint as the flaming sword prevented any return to his former life. He felt pain in his bones. Weakness invaded his body.

Adam had failed his world, his yet-to-be-born children, and his wife. Most of all, Adam had failed his God. He had only himself to blame. No amount of time could undo what Adam had done. No amount of working the soil could remove the guilt that now stalked him every night. His descendants would forever remember his name alongside those sad descriptors: Adam…sin…and death.

"For as in Adam they all die" (1 Cor 15:22).

But the father of all the living doesn't sit alone in disgrace under the star-filled sky. You sit there with him. The same feelings of guilt wash over you, too. Similar failures haunt your memories. You have failed your family as a father, as a mother, as a child, as a worker, and as a servant. During the day you can get lost in work. Sports and reading and travel and music can partially drown out guilt's cry in your heart. But then comes the night, when silence causes your mind to echo with the sound of your sins.

You have felt them too, haven't you? You punished your children too severely. Try as you may, you cannot remove that memory. You remain unable to make up for it. You lost your job. Your ability to provide for your family now rests in the hands of someone else—a failure that churns deep within your soul. You caused someone else in your family to fall into sin—a mistake that has now pulled others down into the pit of dangerous consequences alongside you. You hear your own sinful words come out of the mouths of your children and wonder deep down if your parenting is doing them more harm than good.

You know what it is like to sit where Adam sits on that most awful of nights. You have felt the guilt that now paralyzes Eve in the evening after her fall. And into that darkness slithers the devil all over again. In this sinful world he gleefully makes himself a constant companion of the brokenhearted. He stokes the fire of grief burning within the hearts of sinners.

That is when the night becomes dangerous. Satan whispers to you: *Take matters into your own hands.* He tells you to place your guilt on others, convincing you to run away from them so that you can somehow outrun your own culpability. Did Adam do that? Did he look away from Eve in an attempt to forget his own shortcomings that day? Did Eve become angry with Adam in a desperate attempt to offload her own guilt onto her husband? Did silence keep them from discussing their sorrows?

Or did Satan turn this first couple inward? Did anger and frustration melt away, leaving behind only sorrow and hopelessness? To know that you have ruined the world might just lead anyone into the depths of despair. And that despair can lead a sinner to end it all. Did Adam consider self-destruction?

Have *you*?

More than anything else, Satan wants you to walk down that road toward destruction. The route from sin to guilt to despair to hopelessness contains many signs and warnings, but he doesn't want you to see any of them. Satan wants you to think you are traveling that path alone.

Initially, Adam and Eve thought they had to travel alone. After they sinned, when they heard the Lord approaching, they attempted to hide from the Lord. Their first solution was to go it alone. Their own guilt felt too terrible to take to the Lord.

But Adam and Eve never traveled alone. The Lord was with them, even when they hid. The Lord escorted them, even when they said goodbye to the Garden of Eden forever. When they gave birth to children in their own image, the Lord helped them. And even during the long nights of grief and guilt, *especially* during those nights, the Lord walked with them.

The fallout from Adam and Eve's sin would continue to haunt them. The Lord remained upfront about that. Painful labor among thorns and thistles would plague Adam's work—and the livelihood of everyone who came after him. Painful labor would accompany Eve whenever she gave birth—and whenever any of her daughters would give birth. Most of all, this sin would lead to death.

"For as in Adam they all die" (1 Cor 15:22).

But an incredible promise superseded even the worst of these consequences. In those final moments in the Garden, the Lord had not just explained these consequences to Adam and Eve. He also pronounced them over Satan as well. "I will put hostility between you and the woman, and between your seed and her seed. He will crush your head, and you will crush his heel" (Gen 3:15).

This first gospel promise was the light that would shine through Adam and Eve's darkest nights. It stood as their sure and certain hope in the midst of their struggle against hopelessness. It was a reminder that they would never walk through their guilt-ridden existence alone. This promise remained a declaration that even though their sin brings death, their Seed—their promised descendant—would bring life.

"For as in Adam they all die…so also in Christ they all will be made alive" (1 Cor 15:22).

That is why Adam could return to Eve after guilt stalked him that first night. That is why Eve could speak to her husband in the calm voice of a loving wife. This promise is what kept the first couple alive in this sinful world. It pointed them to the next one.

This promise stands as your sure and certain hope, too. No guilt can defeat it. Not one sin can overcome it. The Seed has come. The Son of God became a son of Adam. He grabbed a hold of every one of your sins. He emptied your heart of grief. He endured every consequence of every trespass. He came to be crushed under them all. And he came to crush the head of your enemy.

This is the light that shines through your black nights of grief, son of Adam. Jesus' death and resurrection brightens your darkest evening, daughter of Eve. The Son of God has not forgotten you. You are not alone. You are *never* alone. He made you a son of your Father in heaven. Do not give up. Take your guilt and place it at the cross. Because at the end of the day, Jesus has saved you. He has saved you from your sins, from your guilt, from your weaknesses, and from yourself.

Comfort for the Night

"Yes, my life is consumed by grief, and my years by groaning. My strength fails because of my guilt, and my bones grow weak. Let your face shine on your servant. Save me in your mercy" (Ps 31:10,16).

CHAPTER 3

Great Darkness Fell Upon Him

Genesis 15:12-20

A man slowly walked through the White House. He heard sobbing coming from the back corridors. He saw people filing through the presidential home with somber faces. Everyone was dressed in black. Finally, after a moment he realized why.

Someone had died.

An ornate wooden casket sat in the middle of the East Room of the White House. The man walked closer, hoping to see just who it was who rested inside. But a guard stood in his way. Curiosity finally got the best of the man. He asked the soldier, "Who is dead in the White House?"

In a low voice the man solemnly replied, "The president." Just before the visitor could ask how such a tragic end could befall a sitting president, the guard answered, "He was killed by an assassin."

Had the man been permitted to move forward and look into the casket he would have beheld a most frightening sight. He would have seen...*himself*.

It was at that moment that President Abraham Lincoln woke up. Thankfully, he was still alive. But the dream stayed with him. How could it not? "Ominous" feelings must have swelled over America's 16th president. Although the North celebrated their recent victory over the South in the nation's Civil War, dark dreams apprehended Abraham Lincoln.

Context reveals just how dark Lincoln's dream really was. He woke up from his nightmare on April 4, 1865. In just 10 days he *would* be assassinated. In 11 days he would lay in state in the East Room of the White House under guard.

Dreams predicting future events always seem ominous. The night before Julius Caesar was assassinated, his wife, Calpurnia had a dream. In it she held her husband's bloodstained body. He had been stabbed to death in the Senate. All she could do was watch in horror, helplessly holding her husband's body.

She woke up, pleading that Caesar not meet with the Senate that day. He wasn't going to go, but then some of his closest friends convinced him to attend anyway. On that day the nightmare became reality. Members of the Roman Senate stabbed Julius Caesar to death.

It is common for Christians to dismiss such dreams as fantastical. Usually they are. But sometimes God himself proclaims the future through frightening dreams. The people he approaches in such dark times are hardly ever the most prominent individuals. They often sit in the peripherals.

During the season of Lent we hear about one of the most memorable and ominous dreams in Scripture. As far as we know she is not a believer. She did not descend from one of the tribes of Israel. She wasn't waiting for the promised Messiah. She was the wife of the Roman governor. And while Pontius Pilate sat in judgment of Jesus, she sends him an ominous message: "Have nothing to do with that righteous man…since I have suffered many things today in a dream because of him" (Matt 27:19).

Pilate refused to listen to the warning. Discarding caution seems to be his legacy. But who could blame Pilate, or Caesar, or Lincoln? Dreams come and go. If we regarded every dream a vision and every dark night a premonition our minds would break from incessant suspicions. Even if God was behind the frightful premonitions, nothing changed. Everyone died who was going to die.

So how is a believer to react to ominous dreams? When we see ourself in the casket, or our loved one lying dead in our arms, how does God want us to react? How can we avoid the fear that comes during our long, ominous nights?

Take a look at the father of our faith. What began as a peaceful sleep quickly turned into terror. "When the sun was going down, a deep sleep fell on Abram. Then terrifying, deep darkness fell on him" (Gen 15:12). The Lord had come to the anxious man in a dream, but Abram couldn't have been feeling any safer at this point.

It was that moment when the dream turned ominous. Pilate's wife and Calpurnia and Abraham Lincoln each knew that moment too well. Perhaps you do, too.

Now, I'm not talking about premonitions, or moments when you felt the storm clouds of the future. That's not really what this devotion is about.

This is what God is asking: Have you felt terrified because tomorrow looked hopeless? Have tears filled your eyes as you sit beside your dying spouse, or parent? Have anxieties so filled your memories that you can't help but dream about "terrifying, deep darkness" (Gen 15:12)?

That was where Abram found himself on a most dreadful night. And the dream only got darker from there. "Know this!" God's booming voice echoed through the walls of Abram's dream. The "stranger in a strange land" was about to find out that his descendants would live under even worse conditions. Yes, he would have children and grandchildren, enough for a future nation! But slavery would define those people for four hundred years.

Hopelessness about the prospects of future generations is nothing new. Abram did not even have a child yet and still the future left him dismayed. Your parents worried about it, too. And yet, here you are. The Lord did not abandon them. He will not abandon you to a hopeless future either.

In his anxiety, Abram attempted to turn his entire estate over to a man named Eliezer of Damascus. It was a legal way for Abram to circumvent his inability to have an heir. But God reminds Abram, and you, that his promises have never been dependent on legal loopholes. And just to hit that point home, the Lord uses a legal procedure to authenticate his promise with Abram. He cuts some animals in half.

The strange scene of dividing a three-year-old heifer, female goat, ram, turtledove and young pigeon might strike us as odd. God doesn't do this anywhere else in Scripture. But then again, no other believer spent as much time in the Babylonian city of Ur as Abraham did. The scene did not look strange to him. If anything, it looked comforting.

For a moment, the foreign hills of Canaan felt like home. Abraham would have recognized that God was using the old Babylonian way of making a covenant. Cutting animals in half, the two parties would walk between them. Every time one of the two who made the covenant would consider reneging on the deal, they were to think back to their memorable footsteps amidst the blood of beasts. Sealed in blood, this agreement remained the strongest a man from Babylon could make.

This land would surely belong to Abram's descendants.

However, nothing in Abram's present life seemed to back up God's proclamation. He had no children. His wife was barren. He owned no property. His descendants would be enslaved in another land by another people. Every night the devil would have reminded Abram of this insurmountable list of shortcomings.

Satan has a way of reminding us of our shortcomings under the cover of darkness. The promises of God can often seem dim in the solitude of a long night.

That's why the Lord took Abram outside. Every night when doubt would creep into his mind he could look to the stars as a reminder of God's promise. "This is what your descendants will be like" (Gen 15:5).

Don't let your dreams perturb you. If God wanted to tell you something through them he would make it crystal clear. But he doesn't need to talk to you that way. You have his Word, which points you to his Son. Your Savior, who took all of your long nights of guilt and sin upon himself, who walked that long Lenten road to Calvary, promises to calm your nights with his presence.

You are not alone. You will never be alone. Your powerful God protects you…even through your long, anxiety-filled nights.

Comfort for the Night

"Do not be afraid, Abram. I am your shield, your very great reward" (Gen 15:1).

CHAPTER 4

You Are A Dead Man

Genesis 20

Does the death penalty keep you up at night? Probably not. I doubt you are reading this on death row. Bars may not currently block your path to the kitchen. Presumably, an executioner does not stalk the hallways of your home, waiting to swing you from a rope.

But death itself might keep you awake at night.

Say what you will about the excruciating wait of the prisoner on death row, at least he knows exactly when death will arrive. We have no such luxury. Death lies in wait, crouching among the reeds, waiting to pounce on us. And death doesn't seem to mind revealing himself. If anything, death's appearance helps fuel our fear of him.

Sleep often eludes the mind that meditates on death. Perhaps that is because the two seem so similar. Whether you like to admit it or not, you act out death nightly as you quietly lay down in darkness, your body immobilized.

The ancient Greeks drew that unnerving comparison between sleep and death. According to their pantheon of gods, Hypnos, the god of sleep, and Thanatos, the god of death, were brothers. If a Greek mother from that ancient world sat next to you right now, she could readily explain to you that you must meet Hypnos on a nightly basis. She would encourage you to happily greet him! Then just as quickly, she would warn you to watch out for his brother, Thanatos.

This close connection between sleep and death has instilled a special type of fear in some people called Hypnophobia. It is the fear of falling asleep. Perhaps you have had your frightful moments of giving yourself over to sleep. Certainly, this acquiescence is a nightly exercise in trust. The expectation is that you will wake up again. This specific fear reminds you that some people don't.

One night, after traveling through a region called the Negev, Abraham slept soundly. It was the sleep of someone who felt like he had complete control over his life. As a rich man living in the land of Canaan, Abraham had acquired a large number of servants and animals. He still didn't have a son to inherit his vast wealth and carry on the family name, but the Lord said he would eventually bless the patriarch with one.

It was a good night for patriarchs. But it was a deadly night for kings. After taking in Abraham's large nomadic band, King Abimelek invited Abraham's sister into his own home. Such an action seemed to be customary. Yet something was amiss.

In the dark of the night, in the middle of a dream, the voice of the Lord boomed into Abimelek's mind, "Listen to me! You are a dead man." Rarely are the Lord's opening words so forceful. Yet there they echoed through Abimelek's head. His dream had become a nightmare. Hypnos was giving way to Thanatos. And why? All for housing a follower of God?

After successfully getting Abimelek's attention, the Lord shines a light on the murky situation. "You are a dead man because of the woman you have taken, because she has a husband" (Gen 20:3). That's not what Abimelek had been told. Upon his arrival, Abraham had pulled a stunt from his days in Egypt. Abimelek couldn't explain the facts quickly enough. "Lord, will you kill even a righteous nation? Didn't he tell me, 'She is my sister'? Even she herself said, 'He is my brother'" (Gen 20:5).

Both Abraham and Sarah had lied to him! Was he really going to die because of their scheming? After all, when the Lord declares you a "dead man," the end feels only a breath away.

Have the lies of a close friend kept the sweet sleep of Hypnos from you? I doubt the Lord has called you a "dead person," but perhaps you feel dead all the same. At its lowest point, a loved one's treachery can make you consider death as an alternative to sleep.

But perhaps that is not you right now. Sleep comes quickly. Death seems distance. Your clean conscience lets you slumber without a second thought. Abraham slept soundly, too. Of course, that didn't mean he was innocent. He simply thought he had gotten away with his sinful plan of self-preservation.

Do others lay awake all night because of your words or actions? Did your biting words cut to the soul of someone you love? Did you push others down to get to your secure position in life? Did your self-preservation leave others exposed?

Later in this account, Abraham will explain the reasons behind his deception. They remain less than convincing. "I did it because I said to myself, 'Surely they do not fear God in this place. They will kill me to get my wife'" (Gen 20:11). The problem with Abraham's excuse was that Abimelek *did* fear God! Not only did God terrify him during the night, but Abimelek honored and respected the true God enough to follow his commands the next morning.

But not everyone does. "Surely they do not fear God in this place" (Gen 20:11). The phrase might as well have described the long night Jesus endured from Gethsemane to Golgotha. Jewish leaders who should have trusted the words of their Lord—the Scriptures that pointed directly to Jesus—now trusted only in own self-preservation. To rid the land of Jesus meant their own self-exultation. Even the Romans might look at them differently once Christ was out of the picture.

Judas' betrayal of Jesus was more than a nightmare. It was his Abraham-like act that put another in the direct path of the Almighty's judgment. His subterfuge meant Jesus was a dead man. Jesus perfectly understood the entire situation. But in love, he did nothing to stop it.

The sleepless night would continue. Hypnos would give way to Thanatos. Jesus would suffer and die to pay the price for Abraham's lies and Abimelek's sins in a way neither ever could. His death would take away the doubts that have caused your sleepless nights and your words that have caused the insomnia for others. To be clear, your sinful self-preservation was vindicated by Jesus' death. He paid off the eternal debt they incurred.

This long night of life often finds us either frightened awake with Abimelek or sinfully asleep like Abraham. Both conditions can bring loneliness. But your Lord wants to remind you that you are not alone. Neither Abimelek nor Abraham were alone that night. While Sarah found herself in a most precarious situation, the Lord protected her from the whims of both men. And because only God can orchestrate such specific details in the minds of men, I'll let him explain it: "I know that you have done this with a sincere heart, so I also prevented you from sinning against me. That is why I did not allow you to touch her."

The Lord knew. He always knows. Secret subterfuge cannot hide from his gaze. Frightened followers cannot be forgotten by your Savior. He is watching over you, even when you feel betrayed. He forgives you, even though you have betrayed others. Confess those sins to your Lord in prayer, like Abraham did. Don't be afraid. Healing is yours through your risen Savior.

Comfort for the Night

"When you lie down, you will not be afraid. When you lie down, your sleep will be pleasant. Do not be afraid of sudden terror, nor of the destruction of the wicked when it comes, because the Lord will be your confidence" (Prov 3:24-26).

CHAPTER 5

Wrestling with God All Night

Genesis 32:22-32

Was there ever a more devious trickster than Odysseus? When the Trojan War threatened to drag on for a second decade, it was Odysseus, the king of Ithaca, that devised the plan to gift a wooden horse to the city. Odysseus concocted the plan to hide Greek men inside the wooden present. And it was Odysseus who told those men to pour out of the massive wooden steed under the cover of darkness and unlock the gates to the city.

Although he did not receive all of the credit, the trickster Odysseus was instrumental in the Greek victory over the city of Troy. Now it was time for the conquerors to return home. Most had not seen their homes and families for a decade, and everyone was eager to return—Odysseus most of all.

Poseidon had other plans. The powerful god of the seas was furious with Odysseus because he had blinded Poseidon's son—the massive cyclops. In a rage the sea winds would forever blow against Odysseus and his men, scattering them onto distant islands controlled by frightening monsters and forbidding mages. What should have been a short sail back to Odysseus' little kingdom turned into a never-ending voyage. In addition to facing off against the giant cyclops, Odysseus and his men had to avoid the alluring—and dangerous—call of the sirens. They sailed through colliding rocks and journeyed through the underworld.

During this decade-long struggle to get home, Odysseus lost every one of his men. He battled against Greek gods and even time itself. It soon started to become clear that even Odysseus could not outsmart Poseidon. He felt doomed to wander the seas forever.

But in the middle of the epic, Odysseus is forced into a harrowing task that exposes a most difficult truth. He contacts the deceased souls in the underworld. One by one his fallen comrades approach him asking about events among the living and the whereabouts of loved ones. Some passed away long ago. Others died because of Odysseus.

Then out of the underworld came the prophecy, the one Odysseus thought he wanted to hear. "A sweet smooth journey home, renowned Odysseus, that is what you seek but a god will make it hard for you—I know—you will never escape the one who shakes the earth."[1]

It all must have been too much to take. At this dark point in his journey, Odysseus was forced to come to grips with the cause of his seemingly endless journey. He could not blame his men, or even the angry god of the sea. No, this unending voyage came about because of his own pride and arrogance. Men had died because of him. It seemed no amount of conniving and trickery could help Odysseus escape.

The patriarch Jacob sewed himself into the same cloth as Odysseus. As night fell, Jacob found himself in quite a predicament. His angry, vengeful brother Esau waited for him across the river with 400 men. Jacob had no fighting men, only wives and children and servants. If a battle broke out, it would be a slaughter.

Then, as tends to happen in great epics, everything paused. Night fell. Jacob rested alone under the stars with only his thoughts to keep him company. He certainly had a lot of life experiences to look back on.

The hushed darkness offered him an opportunity to think back to how his situation had become so dire. Even as a child in Isaac's household, Jacob seemed to have a trick up his sleeve for every problem. For a time, everything fell his way. Jacob had deceived his blind father into blessing him instead of his brother Esau. Then he duped Esau into handing over his oldest-brother birthright.

But during this longest of nights, a plan for pacifying his vengeful brother eluded Jacob. It probably felt like no one in his family trusted him anymore. They sent Jacob away on an odyssey that would intrigue even a Greek audience. Jacob's uncle, Laban, tricked him into marrying both of his daughters, Leah and Rachel. Jacob used his wits to get Laban's best animals for himself. Years rolled along. Tempers flared between his wives. Eventually, Jacob's bag of tricks ran out.

---

[1] *The Odyssey*, Robert Fagles (New York: Penguin Group, 1996), 252.

So, there he lay, all alone, thinking over his choices and the heartache they caused. Tomorrow his brother Esau may very well fight to take back his birthright. Jacob's entire family could be brutally put to death. No wonder Jacob was "terrified and very distressed" (Gen 32:7).

Does Jacob's voice speak to you? We like to think that our own wits can get us out of any predicament. Our skill and athleticism can deceive us into thinking that we can escape any disaster we make for ourselves. Sometimes the Lord has to corner us in the night in order to prove to our sinful nature that we cannot save ourselves.

That's what he did to Jacob. His family had crossed the Jabbok. He divided his possessions. He was all alone. Then, all of a sudden, he wasn't. A man came out of the shadows and wrestled with Jacob all night. But this was no ordinary man. This was God himself wrestling the trickster. He had heard Jacob's humble prayer for protection and deliverance—a prayer that held God to his promises.

God's answer to Jacob's prayer stands as a far greater comfort than any answer from the Greek underworld. Our true God gives no hidden meanings. He doesn't need to speak through our dead relatives. Instead, he personally arrives at Jacob's lonely campsite to wrestle with the man who wrestled with the world.

Then the almighty God of the universe threw the match.

After throwing Jacob's hip out of joint, Jacob responded the way any wrestler would—he held on to his opponent for dear life. Then Jacob took the match one step further: "I will not let you go unless you bless me" (Gen 32:26). Jacob's bold, persistent approach pleased the Lord so much that he did indeed bless him. Then the Lord saved him. The next day, the Lord led Esau to raise his arms as a loving brother rather than a sworn enemy. The family wounds had healed—no trickery required.

Long journeys can be arduous affairs, but sometimes they have spectacular endings. The people of Odysseus' kingdom thought he was dead. His wife, now a widow, had to keep her suitors at bay. Every rich guy in the kingdom arrived, intending to marry the queen and rule Ithaca. But it couldn't just be any man. In true Greek-epic fashion, the city of Ithaca would go to the man who could string Odysseus' old bow and shoot an arrow through the rings on twelve mounted axes.

Needless to say, no one was able to do it. Even if someone could string Odysseus' bow—a very difficult thing to do—no one came close to shooting an arrow through the twelve tiny rings atop those axes.

Then an old man walked in. Nobody knew who he was. He walked across the room, grabbed the bow, and easily strung it. Then he picked up an arrow, moved his aged, gray hair aside, and shot... perfectly threading the needle through all twelve rings.

Immediately, everyone in the room looked back over to the old man, who was now young again. It was Odysseus. He was back from the dead!

You know of an even more spectacular return—a return that really happened. The Savior who died for the sins of the world did not remain hidden away in the underworld. He doesn't speak through empty mystical musings. His return marked the most spectacular miracle the world has ever seen. Your Savior, Jesus, rose again from the dead!

He comes to you during your long, nightly journeys. He bids you put aside your own trickery and selfish deceptions. Instead, he tells you to wrestle with him in prayer—the way Jacob did. And hear those beautiful promises that light up the darkness of your hardships. Because in Christ...

Comfort for the Night

"You have fought with God and with men, and you have won" (Gen 32:28).

CHAPTER 6

Joseph's Moment of Truth

Genesis 43:30-31

A few years ago, a 90 year-old German man shuffled into a courtroom. He had lived a life that was more eventful than he cared to admit. He entered the halls of justice - but not to watch a trial. He was on trial. His name was Oskar Gröning, and he was charged with accessory to murder.

He couldn't deny it.

75 years earlier, he had served as a Nazi officer at Auschwitz - one of the concentration camps used to exterminate the Jewish people during World War II. It had taken 3 quarters of a century, but justice finally caught up to him. He was about to get what he deserved for the crimes he committed - the *murder* he accomplished. The judge ruled him guilty.

He certainly was.

For 75 years he had felt guilty. Shame weighed him down. Not a day went by that he didn't think of those people he hurt and killed; the families he separated; the incurable harm he caused.

Everyone seemed to be in agreement. When you find a Nazi, even one as old as Oskar Gröning, you convict him and sentence him to prison...or even better—to death.

That's what you do to the enemy, isn't it? You find him. You accuse him. You sentence him to prison for life...or you sentence him to death. And you don't look back. After all, they are the enemy. They should feel pain. They should receive their comeuppance.

So, what was Egypt's second-in-charge to do when he saw his enemies bowing before him? Joseph had experienced quite a change of fortune since these bowing brothers sold him into slavery. In fact, Joseph's brothers didn't even recognize him. But Joseph recognized them. This was now the second time he had seen them. But this occasion was different. They had brought his brother Benjamin with them.

It was all too much for Egypt's leader to take. Overwhelmed by the situation, Joseph hurried himself into his private chamber. All alone, having just seen the brothers who had betrayed him, having seen his own brother, Benjamin, with his own eyes for the first time in years, Joseph wept.

This point in Joseph's life stood as a watershed moment. As tears streamed down his cheeks he considered his next move carefully. This pause in Joseph's day probably felt like an eternity.

Joseph had experienced this before. Time must have seemed to stand still during those nights when the sun, moon and stars bowed to him in his dreams, or when everyone else's sheaves of grain bended low to his. God was fulfilling those childhood dreams in the other room at that very moment.

Everything must have stopped when Joseph sat in the bottom of the well, overhearing his brothers coldly deciding his fate as they ate their lunch above him. The nights must have felt long as Joseph pushed away any thoughts of adultery in Potiphar's house. The stillness of Egypt's prison must have worn on into an eternity for the wrongly accused son of Jacob. Perhaps there were even moments when Joseph questioned whether or not those dreams he interpreted for Pharaoh would actually come true. If they didn't, he would probably have been put to death.

But the dreams did come true. Now Joseph hid himself from everyone as he wept.

The Lord gives you backroom moments, too. When was the last time the world stood still around you? Perhaps you feel that way right now—the world has paused, nothing moves, and there you are weeping. Do you have brothers like Joseph? Have you wept over the betrayal of someone you trusted? We have all had a close, personal friend cut us to the heart.

If you sit where Joseph sits, then you also face the choice that Joseph faced. Do you respond with vengeance? Most in this world would not bat an eye if you reciprocated with a betrayal of your own. Satan would love to help you enact it, or at least watch you try. Even the thought of retribution is enough to fall into sin.

Sitting in Egypt's royal backroom with Joseph we sometimes consider rising to rebellion, looking to lop off the heads of our enemies as they kneel before us...at least in our minds. We have lashed out against our betrayers with words that strike more painfully than any dagger.

Joseph had been sold into the lowest form of slavery by the very brothers who should have loved him the most. For the exchange of Joseph's life, the brothers received 20 pieces of silver. Perhaps if they had to, they would have given him away for free.

The going rate for betrayal had not changed much in two millennia. When Judas agreed to betray his teacher, Jesus, into the hands of his enemies, he received 30 pieces of silver for the trouble. It was a handsome sum. Unlike Joseph's brothers, Judas would not have to share it with anyone.

In the end, it wasn't enough. Even that large amount of money could not buy off Judas' guilty conscience. Throwing it back into the temple, Judas ran out into the tear-filled night and hung himself.

There would be no last minute rescue for the Son of God. Betrayed by Judas, abandoned by his disciples, hated by his rulers and bludgeoned by Roman soldiers, Jesus stood a man apart from the world. On Calvary he suffered a world's worth of sins. Your every betrayal, your every thought of retribution, each one of your cutting words washed away. The King of the world gave his life to remove our sins.

Just think of all the ways Jesus *could* have carried out vengeance against those who had wronged him. He could have called legions of angels to wipe out the soldiers. With a word he could have sent his false-accusers to hell. With the simplest of motions he could have flicked away his fleeing disciples forever. Yet what does your suffering Savior declare from the cross? "Father, forgive them" (Luke 23:34). And you are forgiven. Even you. Even me. Criminals though we are, guilt-ridden though we may feel. You are forgiven.

And now just as importantly, you get to forgive those around you. The woman who betrayed you...*Father, forgive them*. The family that wants nothing to do with you and what you believe...*Father, forgive them*. The man who took something dear from you...*Father, forgive them*.

After his somber moment alone, Egypt's highest foreign-born son returned to the room. They ate and he sent them away. But hidden inside one of their bags was a cup, a reason to make them return. Perhaps it was a final test to make sure his brothers had amended their lives.

Judah passed the test. Standing up for his brother, Benjamin, in whose sack the cup was found, Judah offered himself up as a slave in Benjamin's place.

It was more than enough.

Finally, the wronged brother left for dead, the betrayed sibling who was sold into slavery revealed himself. This Egyptian leader was their brother, Joseph. No retribution remained in his heart, only forgiveness. A family broken by betrayal now healed together.

Betraying brothers found forgiveness in Egypt, but what about Nazis in Germany?

Of all the people seeking the death of Oskar Gröning, that Nazi war criminal, one woman was perhaps most justified. Her name was Eva Kor. Eva was an Auschwitz survivor. Gröning had watched as Eva's parents and her two older sisters had been killed. And now that Gröning was on trial for his crimes, Eva traveled over to Germany to see him face to face. Everyone who knew this woman must have wondered just how strong her words toward this man would be. How could they not be? He was, at least in part, responsible for the death of her entire family!

What would you say? A final, parting shot? Would you give him an angry slap across the face? Or maybe you would just watch as this old man feels his soul torn apart in the courtroom, as evidence mounts against him, slowly pushing him to prison...or even execution. After all, it is what he deserves.

Eva Kor, her family's sole survivor of Auschwitz, finally met Oskar Gröning face to face. She went right up to him, raised her arms up...and hugged him. Then she said the three hardest words she would ever say..."I forgive you."

And if Eva could forgive Oskar, if Joseph could forgive his brothers, if Jesus could forgive you, then you can forgive also...even your enemy.

Comfort for the Night

"Forgive, just as Christ forgave you" (Col 3:13).

CHAPTER 7

Egypt's Longest Night

Exodus 12:29-36

There was a custom in Egypt around 1446 BC. A Hebrew man would approach the Pharaoh. With the utmost etiquette he would relay the command of his God: "Let my enslaved people go." The Pharaoh would refuse. A plague would wrack the kingdom. The Pharaoh would relent, pleading for mercy. The plague would cease. Pharaoh would respond by hardening his heart.

This custom did not last long—weeks perhaps—but it was consistent. After the water turned to blood, and then back again; after the frogs and the flies and the locusts subsided; once the diseases departed and the darkness dispersed, Moses approached Pharaoh. The leader of Egypt always gave the same customary response. He was nothing if not consistent. He refused to let God's people go.

But even Egypt's powerful Pharaoh could not stand on ceremony forever. A ritual-breaking catastrophe approached. It would be far more disastrous and far more tragic than any plague that preceded it. To announce the advent of this cataclysm, the Lord followed this Egyptian custom one last time. On this tenth and final occasion, Moses approached Pharaoh and explained the parameters of the Lord's imminent judgment.

"About midnight I will go throughout Egypt, and every firstborn in the land of Egypt will die" (Exod 11:4-5). Not one Egyptian family would escape this onslaught of death. Egypt had always had a preoccupation with the grave. Now death would stalk each of them, "from the firstborn of Pharaoh, who sits on his throne, to the firstborn of the female slave who is behind the hand mill" (Exod 11:5).

Egypt has witnessed many frightening terrors throughout her history. Famine and disease have stolen away the lives of countless young Egyptians. Conquering armies have overrun her borders with seeming regularity. Egypt has shed no small amount of tears. But the night of this tenth plague would be her worst. "There will be a loud outcry in the entire land of Egypt, unlike anything that happened before or anything that will take place again" (Exod 11:6).

Still standing on ceremony, Pharaoh's hard heart refused to listen. Then the end came. Death silently descended upon every home of Egypt. Children asleep in bed never awoke. Firstborn parents fell, never to rise again.

Initially a still silence covered Egypt. It was the cold, breathless quiet that hovers in mortuary basements. In one night the Lord had turned a nation fascinated with death into a crypt of dead bodies. Then came the weeping. It was a flood of tears larger than the Nile itself. No Egyptian family avoided the sorrow that death brought that night.

Yet even during Egypt's darkest night, custom survived. As screams echoed off Egypt's massive tombs, Pharaoh summoned Moses. It would be the last time the two stood in the presence of one another. Pharaoh had finally had enough. This final terrible plague had made his stone cold hard heart crack and bleed for his lost son.

"Get up" (Exod 12:31). Most translations render Pharaoh's words as an exclamation. Perhaps they were. But defeat must have oozed from his mouth. Whispers can be angry too.

"Get away from my people!" (Exod 12:31). It had taken ten plagues, cost thousands of lives and instilled a generational fear, but this moment in the night finally arrived. "Both you and the Israelites, go, serve the Lord, as you have said!" (Exod 12:31).

Some countries of this world may still have their worst days coming. Not Egypt. Her worst night is behind her.

Is your worst night behind you? I know for a fact you have stood where the Pharaoh of Egypt stands in Exodus chapter 12. Sinful pride and arrogance have led to consequences you can no longer endure. Perhaps those repercussions are completely justified. You sit up at night rocking a baby to sleep with no spouse to help. You silently mull over the words you used to push everyone you love away...perhaps forever. Maybe tomorrow will bring legal retribution because of your sinful actions. Maybe you have broken the trust of someone you dearly love. Sin so easily becomes our custom, our protocol. You are a sinner like me, like Pharaoh, on that darkest of evenings. I have stood in those grave-like environs too.

But perhaps you are also enduring a tragedy that has nothing to do with your sins. The fallout of living in a sinful world has shaken the once-strong walls of your life into rubble. The one you love has died. Someone close to you has broken your trust. You are not looking forward to standing up to someone who has wronged you. Maybe right now you are looking on helplessly as your child suffers from a sickness. To endure those hardships is to stand where Moses stood.

Think of that difficult place where Israel's leader found himself. Egypt had raised Moses as an adopted son. Her teachers gave the Hebrew boy the best education in the world. She pulled him out of the reeds and made him her child. Now all Moses could do was watch as Pharaoh's hard heart the kingdom apart.

In such times of grief even believers are tempted to question God's justice. Even worse, we are persuaded to question God's love. Where was God's love during Egypt's longest night? How could God's justice allow Egyptian children to die for the sins of their leader? These are the results of a sinful world led by unbelieving people.

But during that night of Egyptian terror God displayed his love in one of Scripture's most poignant displays. Death permeated Israel that night, too. Not the blood of fathers and mothers and children, but the blood of lambs. Every family that painted their doorposts with the blood of the lamb was passed over by God's angel of death.

On Egypt's worst night, God's love pointed his people to the world's worst day. The Lamb of God would come. Not a bone of this unblemished Lamb would be broken. His blood would stain the wood of his cross so that eternal death would pass over you. This salvation, your salvation, was always more than just a custom for your Lord. It stands as his promise fulfilled for you.

And yet still, "In the evening, weeping comes to stay through the night" (Ps 30:5). Perhaps your longest evening is yet to come. You may wait up all night over the bed of a loved one close to death. You might watch helplessly as sickness grabs your child. Others may bring consequences on themselves that you wish you could help them avoid.

Weeping comes in those moments. But soon comes the sun. "In the morning, there is rejoicing!" (Ps 30:5).

The night of Egypt's death became the Hebrews' song of life. "You turned my mourning into dancing. You removed my sackcloth and clothed me with joy" (Ps 30:11). Maybe that joy is coming tomorrow. Perhaps it is still a long way off. But an eternity of joy already belongs to you. The long night of this world will eventually give way to the light of your salvation. It was won for you by a Lamb. He shed his blood. He suffered your sins. He healed you. He will continue to strengthen you through the difficult and the delightful, the momentous and the mundane, through death and into life.

Comfort for the Night

"O Lord my God, I cried out to you, and you healed me. Lord, you snatched my life from the grave. You kept me alive so I did not go down into the pit" (Ps 30:2-3).

CHAPTER 8

Trapped

Exodus 14

The ancient Chinese general, Sun Tzu, wrote these words a millennium after the Israelites left Egypt: "When you surround an army, leave an outlet free. Do not press a desperate foe too hard. Such is the art of warfare."[1] Most commanders would agree with the general. An enemy army hoping to escape may take flight and not fight. Pursue them and you just might win a complete victory. But if that enemy army cannot see an escape? They will viciously bite and claw at you like an animal with its back to the wall.

Sun Tzu's advice to you as a soldier is simple: Don't let that happen. Give your enemy the hope of an escape, lest he rush back at you with nothing to lose.

On the shores of the Red Sea the Lord gave his people no such hope. Pharaoh didn't either. The joy of salvation the Israelites felt as they skipped out of Egypt must have seemed so distant now. A great sea stood in front of them. A powerful army rushed against them. Now the crowds of fathers and mothers, children and animals could only huddle in horror as certain death rolled toward them. They were the animal. Their back was against the wall.

But there was no fight left in them. How could there be? The Israelites had not marched out to battle. As far as we know not a single man had equipped himself with a weapon. Even if they had, these were not trained fighters. All they could do was make bricks. And they had neither the time nor the materials to build a wall.

---

[1] Sun Tzu, *The Art of War* (New York: Barnes & Noble Classics, 2003), 34.

That's when the Lord became a wall for his people. As Pharaoh's war machines roared closer to God's people, the Angel of God stepped between them (Exod 14:19). No bricks were needed. Weapons became useless. The thickest cloud the world had ever seen now separated a crowd of scared slaves from the mightiest army in the world.

All night the cloud separated the prey from their predators. But the two sides saw a vastly different sight. "The cloud was dark on one side, but it lit up the night on the other" (Exod 14:20). Egypt sat in darkness. God's children stood in light. No wonder then that, "Neither group approached the other all night long" (Exod 14:20).

Why? God's miraculous, upcoming water-crossing certainly wasn't contingent on having enough time. As always, the Lord's timing was perfectly planned for his people. It was a blustery night. "All night long the Lord drove the sea back with a strong east wind and turned the sea into dry land" (Exod 14:21).

All God's people could do was sit and, as Moses put it, "wait quietly" (Exod 14:14). I suppose we could call this a "timeout." Every father, mother, child and grandparent could spend the night thinking about God's goodness. Yes, on the other side of the cloud was an army waiting to cut them all to pieces. Yes, they were the trapped crowd that Sun Tzu warned against. And yes, a massive body of water stood before them...and a hostile wilderness beyond that. But none of that was to be their concern at the moment. The Lord stopped them in their tracks. He gave them the entire night to rest and meditate.

The psalm was written many years later, but I wonder if Psalm 77 is meant to place her readers and singers on those banks of the Red Sea that night. "With my voice to God—with my voice I cried out to God, and he listened to me. In the day when I was distressed I sought the Lord" (Ps 77:1).

How can we not think of Moses as the psalmist writes, "At night my hand was stretched out, and it never grew tired, but my soul refused to be comforted. God, I remembered and I groaned. I pondered, and my spirit became weak" (Ps 77:2-3).

Sometimes, as night keeps your troubler at bay, all you can think about is the heartache, the sadness or even the destruction that morning will bring. You simply want to close your eyes like a distressed child, hoping your enemy won't come if you cannot see him. The psalm writer must have been attempting that very same tactic.

"You propped my eyelids open. I was troubled but did not speak" (Ps 77:2-4).

Our sinful hearts often jump between trust and doubt during long, dark hours like these. "Will the Lord reject forever? Will he never again show favor? Has his mercy vanished to the end?" (Ps 77:7-8).

As the enemy waits for you those pleas of the psalmist might just spill out of your heart, too. Which of your enemies is waiting to pounce on you when the sun rises? Who frightens you so completely that your spirit becomes weak? "All armies prefer high ground to low and sunny places to dark,"[2] Sun Tzu writes. And that includes us, too.

But sometimes the Lord purposefully brings you right down into those darkened valleys of your life. He lets your enemies become too numerous. He allows your situation to become dire. He makes you feel weaker than you have ever felt.

In those awful moments God knows exactly how you feel. In fact, he experienced far worse. Caught between the red hot anger of his Jewish leaders and the cold indifference of Roman soldiers, Jesus suffered the long night of abandonment on the cross. Armies may prefer high ground, but not our Savior. He descended into the depths to take upon himself our hellish punishment. Generals prefer sunlight to darkness. Not Jesus. He turned the sun black as he suffered for your sins.

His weakness becomes your strength. His death means your life. His darkness becomes your daylight.

In the still dark of your night, Jesus whispers to you through the words of Moses, the man caught in the middle. He whispers to you from his word, "Wait quietly." God's Word strengthens feeble hearts even during the blackest of nights. "I will remember the deeds of the Lord. Yes, I will remember your wonderful work from long ago. I will meditate on all your work, and I will ponder all your deeds" (Ps 77:11-12).

Aren't those the truths that God wanted his huddled families to remember on the banks of the Red Sea that night? Plague after plague had destroyed Egypt. Each Egyptian false god bowed to the real power of the true God. "You are the God who performs a wonderful deed. You made known your power among the peoples. With

---

[2] Sun Tzu, 140.

your arm you redeemed your people, the descendants of Jacob and Joseph" (Ps 77:14-15).

The night sky continued to blow violently above everyone. "The sound of your thunder was heard in the tornado. Lightning lit up the world. The earth trembled and quaked" (Ps 77:18).

Finally, morning came. Waters roared. Mud dried. "Your route led through the sea. Your trail went through the mighty waters" (Ps 77:19). After one of the longest nights of their lives, fathers and mothers, children and grandparents slowly rose up. Their journey would take them on a path no one had ever walked. A path straight through the sea gave Israel what they had hoped for…a way out.

More lonely temptations stood on the horizon. That's how our sinful nature works. Miracles fade into the past. Present sufferings blind us to God's big salvation picture. Future worries steal away our focus. The cloud and the fire don't always appear ahead of us. Sometimes we feel as though we walk alone…especially at night.

But listen to how the psalmist ends his song. It might just have been where Moses would have ended it: "O God…your footprints were not detected. You led your people like a flock by the hand of Moses and Aaron" (Ps 77:19-20).

Don't look for the footprints. The Lord chooses not to leave those behind. He does that on purpose to give you yet another opportunity, even during this wind-whipped night, to trust.

He will give you a way out—not to conquer you, but to save you.

Carry Moses' words with you when the enemy stands over you, when the terrors of night threaten you with doubt.

Comfort for the Night

"Do not be afraid. Stand firm, and see the salvation from the Lord, which he will perform for you today. For the Egyptians you see today, you will never see again. The Lord will fight for you. You must wait quietly" (Ex 12:13-14).

CHAPTER 9

On the Rival's Roof

Joshua 2

Two men received a secret summons. Their commander, Joshua, was sending them on a mission. No one in their right mind would have signed up for this assignment. "Go and look over the land" (Josh 2:1). That appeared to be easy enough. But then at the end of the command, almost as an afterthought, Joshua added, "…and Jericho" (Josh 2:1).

Not only were these men to secretly spy out an entire land, with the future lives of countless soldiers hanging in the balance, but they were to also specifically investigate the city of Jericho. If the kings of Canaan were like hostile European kingdoms, then Jericho stood as their impenetrable Gibraltar—a separate, unconquerable rock of a city.

Humanly speaking, Joshua's secret mission represented so many things that were wrong with God's Canaanite conquering campaign. One does not simply waltz into a fortress of a land inhabited by giants. If success is to come, then rules must be followed.

The Ten Commandments for Conquering Canaan
1. Do not attempt to take over the land with a young, inexperienced generation.
2. Do not cross the Jordan at flood stage.
3. Do not circumcise your fighting men on the eve of your campaign.
4. Do not begin your operations by trying to conquer Jericho.
5. Do not bring along women and children; only fighting men.

6. Do not let the kings of the Amorites unite against you.
7. Do not expect to quickly conquer a land of fortified cities guarded by giants.
8. Do not let your spies tell the people how difficult a prospect your war will be.
9. Do not trust any Canaanite person to help you.
10. And whatever you do, make sure not to enter the land unless the Lord goes with you.

Most commanders would agree on these commandments. Proper preparation and good sense must prevail if an army such as Israel's intends to win a battle—let alone a war—against Canaan.

And yet what does God tell his people to do? He has Joshua break almost every one of these humanly constructed commandments!

1. He let the first generation—the one with the most invested—die out before beginning a conquest (Num 14:29).

2. He told his people to cross the Jordan River at flood stage (Josh 3:15-17).

3. God circumcised every able-bodied man right before going into battle (Josh 6:2-3).

4. The Lord told Joshua to begin his campaign by taking Jericho (Josh 6:1-2).

5. God brought not only men who could fight, but women and children who could not (Josh 6:10-11).

6. The kings of the north (Josh 10:5) and the kings of the south (Josh 11:5) united against the Israelites.

7. The Lord had Joshua conquer Canaan quickly (Josh 11:23).

8. Moses had his spies share just how difficult conquering Canaan would be (Num 13:31-33).

9. The lives of Joshua's spies depended on the kindness of a Canaanite prostitute named Rahab (Josh 2).

10. The first time Israel invaded the promised land, they did so without the Lord. After being told not to invade Canaan because of their insolence, some Israelites went anyway and were utterly destroyed (Num 14:39-45).

How would Joshua's Israelites act? If the experience of his two spies foreshadowed how the invasion would proceed, then the situation appeared dicey. No sooner had the spies entered the fortress city of Jericho then the gates were shut and guards began searching for them.

So far, the spies had been living out a veritable "what-not-to-do" when it came to spying out the land. But contrary to everyone's expectation, a foreigner helped them. Her name was Rahab. She was a prostitute.

During the night she took the two men and hid them among the flax stalks on her roof. Soldiers rushed everywhere. The massive gate shut. The spies were trapped behind enemy lines. Their only hope rested on a woman who worked in a most dubious profession.

Time must have slowed to a stand-still that night on the roof. Lying in wait can be the most difficult maneuver. When every instinct tells you to run for your life, doing nothing can feel counter-intuitive...maybe even impossible.

If the jaws of the monstrous land of Canaan began at Jericho, these men were stuck between her teeth. This is when the devil crouches down, hurling doubts and fears into the minds of poor surrounded souls. Alone with their thoughts, those two spies must have heard the doubts slink into their minds. "How can our people hope to capture this castle town? We can't even escape it!"

Fear must have welled up within them. It must have shown on their faces.

By the time Rahab came to the roof, they must have thought it was all over. Why else would she come up but to indicate to the guards where they were? After all, when death hangs overhead, don't prostitutes choose save their own lives?

Are you sitting on the roof of a great Jericho? Do you feel as though enemies have surrounded you and you cannot trust anyone? The battles of this world often look like this. Physically, your life might look fine to the outside world. But what about your spiritual situation? Countless enemy angels surround you, looking for a way to drag you down to hell. Your lion of an enemy, the devil, lies in wait, hoping to rip your faith away. Your sinful nature works on you from the inside, pointing out all of your woes and getting you to question God's love in such distressing times. And the world around you refuses to believe that any of these enemies even exist.

Jericho stands before you tomorrow…and the next day…and the next. And just when you are ready to give up, just when the prostitute climbs up to the roof you are hiding on, everything appears to be over.

But it isn't all over.

Rahab did not climb onto the roof to "out" the spies. She came to make an announcement—perhaps one of the most surprising in the entire Bible. "I know that the Lord has given you the land. Because of you, terror has fallen upon us, and all the inhabitants of the land are melting in fear before you" (Josh 2:9).

Really? The only terror that seemed to exist resided in the minds of those two spies. Instead, the giants living behind the strongest walls of Canaan feared a group of wandering families from the wilderness. Just when the situation seemed most dire, the Lord revealed his most glorious and loving truth. Even giants fear the Lord. Even the strongest of walls cannot withstand God's almighty power. Even Canaanite prostitutes can be brought to faith.

Miraculously, those spies escaped Jericho unharmed. They safely arrived back among their fellow Israelites. And with one of the most profound spy reports in the history of mankind, the two men shared the situation ahead: "The Lord has without doubt given the entire land into our hands" (Josh 2:24).

The Lord purposefully broke the first nine of those ten commandments for conquering Canaan. He had to. It would be the only way his people could follow that tenth commandment for conquering the land. They needed to learn to fully trust in the Lord rather than themselves. During their long night on Rahab's roof those spies learned a lesson they would not soon forget.

We need to continue learning that lesson. Sometimes God reminds us of those profound truths from the most unlikely people. A Canaanite prostitute speaks courage into a couple of scared spies. A stranger reminds you that you are not alone. A comment from a friend who hasn't been in church for a while points you back to the truth of God's Word.

The Jerichos of this world still stand before you. The only way you can face them with confidence is through faith in Christ, your Savior. You cannot prevail against them alone. But take heart, because you are not alone! Jesus faced hell itself. He took your cross and your sins and your death. He rose to life to assure you of his power. It is a power that stands even over death.

Now he walks with you into battle…reminding you that he has already won your victories.

Comfort for the Night

"Be strong and courageous. Do not be terrified and do not be overwhelmed, because the Lord your God is with you wherever you go" (Josh 1:9).

CHAPTER 10

Gideon's Night of Locusts

Judges 7:9-22

Have you heard of Clare Hollingworth? Don't feel bad if you haven't. Not too many people recall her anymore. But even if you don't know anything about Clare, you probably know what she found. Clare had just started her employment in a business where people are sent out to find things. She was a reporter—newly minted and working for the *Daily Telegraph*.

It was her first week on the job. No doubt she was still searching for her voice as a writer, still finding her footing as a reporter. But whether she was ready or not, in her first week of reporting Clare was driving a car along the border between Germany and Poland. That's where she found what most journalists search their entire lives to find.

Over a ridge she saw a massive force of German tanks and soldiers preparing to march on Poland. The invasion would mark the beginning of World War II, but at this point the only people who knew about it were those hardened German troops, the Führer—Adolph Hitler...and Clare Hollingworth.

At first no one believed her. Perhaps they viewed her as a young reporter trying too hard to make a name for herself. Maybe they thought she mistook the Polish army for the Germans. In order to fully prove her situation, she later held out the phone from her room's window. Hearing the sounds of the German forces, the British embassy was convinced. Soon the world found out what Clare Hollingworth stumbled into—Germany was invading Poland.

To this day, we call Clare's discovery "the scoop of the century."

Imagine wandering through the hills as an Israelite making your way from one cave hideout to another. Then over the next ridge, seemingly out of nowhere, stands a force as numerous as a cloud of locusts. Midianites and Amalekites were now in the middle of Israel. They had arrived in full force.

You quickly run back to your family's hidden cave, hoping one of these locusts doesn't track you down. Would your family believe your news? Perhaps not the first time it happened. You probably mistook the Israelite army for a Midianite one.

And there you stand, in the darkness of the cave, sharing the "scoop of the century" and nobody believes you.

Eventually, even the most vehement Israelite doubter had to admit the reality of this astounding Midianite force. But what could they do? Israel precariously stood on the brink of annihilation, like Poland on the eve of World War II.

But God had a savior in mind, and he would be one of the least likely heroes in Scripture. One day the Lord found a man named "Gideon" hidden away in a winepress. That's how bad the situation had become in Israel. God's people had to secretly thresh wheat where wine used to be made.

Gideon was as surprised as anyone that the Lord had chosen him and not someone else. Maybe he simply wished God would have chosen someone else. After all, in their first conversation Gideon answers God's summons by saying, "How can I deliver Israel?" (Judg 6:15). He was too small; his country was too weak to do anything.

But he also had a nagging question, one that might sound all too familiar. "If the Lord is with us, why has all this happened to us?" (Judg 6:13). How indeed?

After that exchange, every word and every sign that God provides Gideon is an answer to this question. How could Gideon expect to survive after seeing the Angel of the Lord? The Lord reminds him, "Do not be afraid. You will not die" (Judg 6:23). How can Gideon really know that the Lord is with him? The Lord douses only Gideon's fleece over night (Judg 6:38). Then, to further prove the point, God douses only the ground around the fleece the following night (Judg 6:40). How can Gideon fully trust in the Lord and not depend on his own number of men? God whittles Gideon's force down to almost nothing (Judg 7:8).

Is the Lord really with me? Gideon must have wondered one final time as night fell on his force of 300 men. A far stronger army stood before them. The Lord doesn't use the phrase very often in the Bible, but here he compared Midian's forces to a flood of locusts. Maybe that didn't even do their numbers justice.

At the very moment when Israel needed her greatest numbers, the Lord sent them all away. Only 300 remained! One among them, Gideon, must have felt temptation knocking on the door of his heart. In his mind he may have felt like he was back where the Lord first found him—in that winepress, secretly threshing wheat. His men might have wished for their safe hideouts deep in the mountain caves.

Sometimes darkness has to descend in our lives to show us just how many locusts have gathered against us. Like Gideon, we gaze out on their individual flickering lights, too numerous to count, too many to vanquish. Then Satan whispers, "If the Lord is with you, why has all this happened to you?"

Why would the Lord reveal to you an army of problems and imminent personal disasters just waiting to invade your life? Why would the Lord allow your situation to seem so very hopeless?

Because if he didn't, you might be tempted to think you could get yourself out alive.

Sometimes the Lord whittles down your options so far that you can no longer trust in yourself. He turns your 22,000 into 300...or fewer. And there you stand, holding a toothpick instead of a tree.

For Gideon, the Lord had to turn out all the lights before he could show Gideon where his true brilliance came from. Going down into the valley, Gideon got close enough to the swarm of enemy soldiers to hear a couple of them talking. Imagine that walk! Crouching down, silently moving he made every effort not to be found. There he witnessed first hand just how impossible the stakes were. No commander in Israel's history had faced such long odds. No man had been asked to do more with less.

And there in the dark, taking it all in was Gideon. That's when he overheard a Midianite man relaying an ominous nightmare. He dreamt a loaf of barley bread crashed into the Midianite tents, destroying them. The vision seemed clear to everyone who heard. But just in case the creeping Gideon missed the message, the Lord restated it to him through the words of one of his enemies: "What can that be but the sword of Gideon son of Joash, the man of Israel. God has given Midian and the whole camp into his hand" (Judg 7:14).

And he was right. Later that night, the horns and torches of Gideon's men sent the Midianites into such confusion that they destroyed each other wholesale. All around them barley bread crashed through tents. It all added up to a most astounding victory for Gideon. And no one could argue that the Lord had done everything.

So, it is for you. Hidden away in your cave, fearing the enemies that surround you, the difficulties waiting on the horizon, you might just understand Gideon's feelings of helplessness. You might even have been asking, "If the Lord is with me, why has all this happened?"

Sometimes the Lord turns out all the lights in order to show you what truly shines. He weakens us to remind us where our strength comes from. To all of these worries, in the face of every fear he shows us his Son, Jesus. His suffering removed our sins. His darkness becomes our light. His death means our life.

It all leads to this timeless promise the Lord has in store for you. Don't shrink away from it. Hold on to it with all of your heart.

Comfort for the Night

"Peace be with you. Do not be afraid. You will not die" (Judg 6:22-23).

CHAPTER 11

Samson's Silent Sacrifice

Judges 16

William Faulkner was a Mississippi man through and through. As an author, his pen permanently attached itself to those southern fields and aristocratic families that he knew so well. He wasn't alone. It seemed each man in the south had a strong connection to the fields they grew up in and the causes they fought for, which is why Faulkner once wrote these famous words: "For every Southern boy fourteen years old, not once but whenever he wants it, there is the instant when it's still not yet two o'clock on that July afternoon in 1863."[1] For most of us, that time and day may not carry significant meaning. But for men like Faulkner, for southern boys to this very day, two o'clock on July 3, 1863, draws them in like no other date.

For generations, boys of the South have transported their minds to that shady glen below the heights of Gettysburg. Each one picks up his gun and silently walks over to the assembling group. Anxious thoughts of an oncoming barrage of shells and the approaching whistle of bullets from enemy guns all wait for their movement.

There they sit, the men of the South. Generation after generation they wait under the trees, ready to make their doomed charge up the hill. No one asks why. Not a man questions the supreme command of the general they admire. They simply wait.

They wait to die.

By the summer of 1863, the Southern Confederacy appeared on the cusp of victory in the North. Up to that point the Civil War

---

[1] William Faulkner, *Intruder in the Dust* (New York: Vintage Books, 2011), 190.

had seen many Confederate victories, but this threatened to be the greatest of them all. Having pushed further north than ever before, Robert E. Lee's seemingly invincible Virginians now saw triumph within their grasp.

But the Northern army held the high ground.

In 1863, at a little town called Gettysburg, the Union army of the north had rushed to halt the advancing Confederacy forces. The first day's fighting had been brutal. Combat on the second day had been a bloodbath. The third day would the worst of them all...at least for one side.

On that last day of the Battle of Gettysburg, General Robert E. Lee remained resolute. He wanted that Union position. He wanted a complete, decisive victory. He wanted the war to be over. He called to one of his generals, George Edward Pickett, to ready his men. They were to make the most fateful charge in southern history.

The wait must have been unbearable. Looking up at the now-silent Union guns established high on a superior position; knowing full well they are about to give their lives in order to take them—how do men operate under such heightened tensions?

You might not be from the south, and maybe you have never been in battle, but perhaps you can mentally walk yourself up to those men sitting in the shade. You don't agree with what they are fighting for, but you can understand their predicament as soldiers. Their fears and apprehensions might just spill over into your heart, too. Most of them have mere moments to live. And they know it.

I don't bring up Pickett's impending charge in order to glorify the Confederate cause. I simply want to place you under the shade of their emotional reckoning. Maybe you already know how gut-wrenching that feels. Perhaps you have been sitting under the shade, waiting for death's inevitable arrival. The doctor has told you the awful news, that treatment will no longer help. Your boss just informed you that they no longer need your services. Your spouse decided to leave. The people at your church who used to welcome you now no longer want you around.

Death comes to us in many forms—the death of our work, the death of our marriage, the death of our friendships, or simply death itself. The depression, the grief, the sadness that ensues can be unbearable. There are times when we no longer feel able to faithfully hold our gun and prepare to meet death—no matter where the battlefield lies.

A frail, blind man hung from chains in prison. He was a southern man awaiting an inevitable death as well. As his Philistine dungeon slowly swallowed him, his broken heart bled out the grief of his tortured soul. He had been betrayed by the one he loved, and he had only himself to blame.

The hands that had once broken gates and ripped apart lions now hung impotently at his sides. Samson had nothing and no one. His parents were long gone. His own Israelite people were happy to be rid of him. And the woman he loved, Delilah, had used him to gain a fortune for herself.

Had he heard the cries of joy outside his cell, he might have noticed that a Philistine celebration would take place the next day. Not only was his capture the reason for these upcoming festivities, he would also be the entertainment.

He had never felt so weak. He had become used to the idea of his own invincibility. But now, like the Confederacy's formerly invisible Virginians below Gettysburg, Samson looked up at death.

Morbid moments like these come to us from time to time, don't they? Joy seems a distant memory. Death seems certain. The end is soon to come.

The world tells you to put on a brave face to meet the situation, but how can you? Your very life may hang in the balance. Often, it is the result of our own failings with sin. Like those Confederates, we have become convinced of our own infallibility. Similar to Samson, we trusted in our own strength and wisdom until it cornered us. No escape, no rescue, just a date with death…or at the very least a meeting with the arrival of judgment against ourselves.

Sin places us in these dark cells. Guilt keeps us covered in darkness. The devil wants to hold us in these black environs forever. Hopelessness remains one of his most powerful illusions. And as we look up at the heights from down below, staring into the face of death itself, hopelessness becomes difficult to shake off.

Are these the emotions Jesus felt as he looked up to the heights of Calvary? Already as a child visiting Jerusalem, did he walk by the "place of the skull" with an ominous heart, knowing the doom that would eventually befall him? Did he consider his death along that road into Jerusalem every time he made the journey? Did he feel Samson's pain as he looked ahead to being the spectacle of his enemies' perceived victory?

Perhaps every Christian can place themselves in Samson's cell on the eve of his death. Dark nights have plagued us as well. But the one location that evades every Christian is Golgotha. We can imagine standing next to Mary and John. We can put ourselves in the place of the onlookers. But try as we may, we will never know what it is like to be the one crucified.

That is by heavenly design. Only Jesus fully knows the suffering, the torment, the hell that our cross brought him. No imagination can duplicate his experience. And while we cannot fully appreciate that suffering, the Lord has given you the faith to believe that it is finished.

Ominous nights still stalk us in this life. Pickett's men understood that better than most. As they gathered to make their ill-fated charge, one of the men, Richard B. Garnett, said to Lewis Armistead, "This is a desperate thing to attempt. The slaughter will be terrible." Armistead replied, "Yes, it is. But the issue is with the Almighty, and we must leave it in His hands."[2] Neither man survived the day.

A terrible day had come for Samson. As the Philistines pushed the feeble man from his cell, Scripture hints that he was not alone. "The hair on his head began to grow" (Judg 16:22).

Then, for perhaps the first time in his life, Samson prayed to the Lord. "Lord God, remember me, I pray. Give me strength, I pray, this one more time, O God" (Judg 16:28). His strength returned just as he was feeling for the two pillars on either side of him. Joyful shouts turned to screams. Celebration morphed into disaster. Thousands died as the structure tumbled down. Samson had given his life for his people.

Jesus gave his life for you. Yes, death will approach. Friendships will end. But in the stillness and silence that precedes those awful moments in your life, take the opportunity to look past the enemy on the heights. See the cross where you salvation was won. You are not alone, even when death comes. You have a Savior who took all of your pain and eternal suffering. And let this comforting verse remind you why...

---

[2] Francis W. Dawson, *Reminiscences of Confederate Service, 1861–1865* (Baton Rouge: Louisiana State University Press, 1980), 96.

Comfort for the Night

"So that through death he could destroy the one who had the power of death (that is, the Devil) and free those who were held in slavery all their lives by the fear of death" (Heb 2:14-15).

CHAPTER 12

Alone in the Dark

Judges 19:11-30

Back in 1974, Marina Abramovic put on a performance unlike any-thing her peers had ever seen. Those who witnessed it firsthand never forgot it. They watched as Abramovic attempted to find the fine line between art and awe.

In her street performance, Abramovic played the simplest of parts. Her role, for six hours, was to stand still. She said nothing. A table stood in front of her, holding 72 different objects. The items themselves ranged from arbitrary to deadly: a rose, brownies, nails, a scalpel, and even a bullet and a gun.

A letter also sat among the items on the table. It shared these instructions with her audience:

Instructions.

There are 72 objects on the table that one can use on me as desired.

Performance.

I am the object.

During this period I take full responsibility.

Duration: 6 hours (8 pm—2 am).

At first, a group of onlookers gathered. Nothing happened. Eventually, a person took the rose and placed it in Abramovic's hand. Another person raised her arms into the air. By the third hour, onlookers had started interacting with Abramovic. Someone touched her. Another person cut all of her clothes off with razor blades. Yet there she stood, completely still, committed to her performance art.

As the hours wore on, the performance slowly turned into a psychological study. How do people react when they begin viewing a person as an object? The gathering crowd was about to find out as one particularly bold individual placed the bullet in the gun, placed it in Abramovic's hand and held it to her head.[1]

Would a person really pull the trigger? Abramovic knew this could be a possibility. After all, she had written on the note "I take full responsibility." But the audacity still shocks us, doesn't it? What type of a person could be so callous that he would blatantly and publicly abuse and kill—or even risk killing—a complete stranger?

Audacious actions like these defined the time of the Judges. They form the visual background to the oft-heard summary of the period: "Every man did whatever was right in his own eyes" (Judg 17:6). In a book that describes long-term wickedness, short-lived repentance and imperfect, selfish judges; one Levite's cold, self-indulgence transcends them all.

He starts out as the victim. It appeared his concubine had been unfaithful and ran out on him. Was she fed up with living as a concubine and not having the rights of a full-fledged wife? Did she love another man? Whatever the case, the Levite eventually travels to the house of his in-laws to convince her to return with him.

The unfaithful concubine's family tried to cover for her desertion through magnanimous hospitality. Day after day the Levite prepared to leave, only to be convinced to stay one more day.

Finally, he had had enough of their hospitality. He got up to leave. But rather ominously, he decided to leave in the evening. As the sun was going down, the Levite went the extra mile and passed the Canaanite-held city of Jerusalem to arrive in Gibeah. No doubt the Levite thought his traveling party would be in good hands among fellow Israelites.

Up to this point, the Levite had been a perfect gentleman, a faithful husband and a caring master. He had brought his concubine back into his household. He had found a safe house owned by an Ephraimite. And even when the still sound of the city erupted into shouts of violence, the Levite seemed to agree with his host that homosexuality was unacceptable.

---

[1] Frazer Ward, *No Innocent Bystanders: Performance Art and Audience* (Lebanon: University Press of New England, 2012), 120.

Then, in a dark scene straight out of a horror film, this Levite gentleman transforms into a monster. The niceties fade away. Hospitality vanishes. He thrusts his concubine into the street and slams the door.

After an unconscionable sleep, the Levite woke up to find his concubine dead on the doorstep. Coldly he kicked her, only to find out she had died at some point in the night. Treating her like an object, he put her on his donkey—along with his other items—and took her body to his butcher shop. With his practiced Levite hand he used his sacrificial knife to cut up her body into enough pieces to send out to the twelve tribes of his people.

This might be the darkest, most vile moment in the entire Old Testament. It sounds so similar to the sounds and screams in the city of Sodom the night Lot and his family ran away. Yet it remains so different. Lot and his family *escaped*. The wicked men did not have their way with the visitors. Justice in Lot's day, as sad as it was, seemed to prevail.

No justice existed in Gibeah. The ravished woman had been unfaithful to her husband. The Ephraimite saved the Levite's party, only to offer his own daughter to the angry mob. And the Levite, who seemed to be the wronged party in the beginning, revealed himself to be the worst of them all.

It can be difficult to identify with anyone in an account like this. But in reality, you can identify with everyone. As awful as it is to admit, dark nights have led you to think unfaithful thoughts or to flee from a promise completely, like that concubine. Maybe you were mad at your spouse. You had an argument with your parent. Perhaps you felt wronged and thought about leaving forever.

You have been that hospitable Ephraimite, ready to do the right thing until your life stood in the way. You have thrown others into danger to save yourself. So often we try to explain our own wickedness in ways that sound logical to our sinful nature. Yet in the end they are still sin.

And then there is that Levite. A cold, calculating man who looked clean on the outside, until his dire situation showed who he really was. Even if it was just in our thoughts, we have sinned in ways that all of these people sinned. We have desired to carry out whatever was right in our own eyes.

That's why Jesus rode to Jerusalem. The outside of the city looked different from the days of the Judges, but her sinful inside was shockingly similar. Hospitable people soon closed their doors to the Savior. Levites coldly wanted him dead, striking him, scourging him, and having him crucified.

And the concubine? She was all of us. Our sins had made us unfaithful to our perfect husband, our Bridegroom. Yet when he could have thrown us out into the cold darkness of an eternity of punishment, he had himself thrust out instead. He was wronged. He was brutalized. He was killed.

His resurrection proves that even our Judges-like sins have been washed away. So have the sins of those who have wronged us in atrocious ways. Jesus came to save all sinners, even the monsters who have committed the most nefarious sins against us.

Marina Abramovic silently stood in a most precarious position. Monsters surrounded her. A loaded gun held in her own hand was about to fire. Her life hung in the balance. That's when a group of spectators rose up. These weren't the selfish cries of wickedness. They were the objections of those who saw her as a person. A fight broke out. The performance ended. Some went up to Abramovic and wiped her tears. Others cleaned up her wounds. One person hugged her.

Abramovic survived.

So have you. You won't always feel like a survivor. There are nights when the world will abuse you and see you as an object. But not your Savior. He knows you by name. He rescued you for all eternity. He will never leave you or abandon you. And one day, he will wipe all of your tears away forever.

Comfort for the Night

"He has swallowed up death forever! The Lord God will wipe away the tears from every face. He will take away the shame of his people throughout the earth" (Isa 25:8).

CHAPTER 13

The Longest Wait of Her Life

Ruth 3:1-15

A woman from the hostile country of Moab crept quietly onto the threshing floor of a prominent Israelite. To the unsuspecting observer the scene might have appeared fraught with danger. Would this woman enact some sort of treacherous revenge on the sleeping man? Could blackmail be on her mind, forcing his hand to give her something in exchange for her silence?

The situation that night on the outskirts of Bethlehem was indeed fraught with danger, but not for the man slumbering on the floor. This foreign woman was putting her very life on the line as she silently approached the feet of the wealthy gentleman, Boaz. This evening would define the rest of her life. If everything went according to the plan her mother-in-law laid out, the townsfolk of Bethlehem would joyfully shout the names of the couple, Boaz and Ruth, in a grand wedding celebration. Ruth very much hoped for this outcome.

But often during the night the mind travels to every negative possibility. Ruth, the foreign woman, had only a slim connection to life in Bethlehem. That connection was her mother-in-law, Naomi. Naomi herself was a widow; her family was as good as dead. No heir lived to inherit her land and continue her family line. Ruth had chosen to leave behind her Moabite family in order to cling to a woman with no perceivable future. Ruth now lived in a land she did not know among a people she might never fully understand.

But all that was yesterday. Tonight Ruth had even more on the line. A man named Boaz had shown her kindness, offering her an opportunity to gather the leftover wheat in the safe environs of his fields. Could his kindness be construed as interest? Naomi dared to think so. Helping her daughter-in-law to get ready for the boldest of proposals, she changed Ruth from the clothes she wore in mourning over her dead husband and into an ordinary robe. She trained Ruth in what to do and what to say.

It appeared Ruth would only have one shot at showing Boaz her desire to marry him. A man like Boaz was rarely alone, especially during night. Only the harvest, a timeframe that came around once a year, offered Ruth a chance at getting Boaz alone. It remained the only time all year when Boaz slept outside by himself on the threshing floor. The opportunity might not come around again for a long time, so Ruth acted with purpose. Silently approaching Boaz, she uncovered his feet.

The negative possibilities must have filled Ruth's thoughts. What if Boaz says "no"? What if he becomes angry at Ruth's boldness and refuses to help her out? What if the gentleman by day turns out to be a monster at night, taking advantage of the woman all alone?

No one knew it that night, but something far more important hung in the balance. The line of the Savior ran through the family of Elimelech and Naomi. Their sons had both died childless in Moab. The wife of one of them, Orpah, stayed behind among her Moabite people. Ruth chose to follow her mother-in-law back to Bethlehem. Humanly speaking, the line of the Savior would live or die with Boaz's reaction to Ruth on this night. Ruth had uncovered his feet. Now all she could do was wait for him to wake up and respond.

How long did Ruth have to wait? The night must have dragged on for an eternity. Lives, livelihoods and the very salvation of mankind all remained suspended in the night air.

What is making you hold your breath? Are you waiting to hear the results from your doctor regarding a recent test? The phone rings and you realize you can't breathe because of the seriousness of the result. The test you spent years educating yourself to take is finally over, but you don't know if you passed until you hear back. Will the answer ever come? Perhaps you stand where Ruth stands, putting yourself out there with a question of "will you marry me," awaiting what feels like an eternity for an answer. Even sending a simple text message can make your heart stop—little moving dots indicating that a response is being written. Will it ever come, or will it just dance in front of you, antagonizing you forever?

Our lungs seem to hold in our fear when breath escapes us. To be sure, our lives may not hang in the balance in just the same way Ruth's did. That doesn't make these breathless moments any less frightening. Fear can still endanger faith, even when the stakes are less than life or death.

In his word, God often compares you and me to an unfaithful bride. Nothing about our sinful situation draws God to us, nor should it. You and I are the foreign woman with nothing to offer him. But where Ruth often proved faithful, we have been by nature faithless. Who would want us? Who would ever redeem us from our hell-bound situation?

And yet, in spite of all of these shortcomings, failings and sins our bridegroom approached anyway. He descended into our world. And being the perfect husband, he took all of the debt our sins incurred and paid the price to set us free. The price was a heavy one. He would have to suffer. He would have to die. In this context of the love a husband ought to show to his wife, Paul reminded the believers in Ephesus: "Christ loved the church and gave himself up for her to make her holy" (Eph 5:25-26).

Hold your breath if you must, as you look upon Christ's cross. His payment brought you into his household. See those moments on Calvary where everything hung in the balance. Walk away from Good Friday the way those disciples must have, when life itself appeared to freeze in place. And then breathe out all those fears and anxieties with the sigh of relief...and hope...and joy...that comes from the empty tomb on that glorious Easter Sunday.

The groom has come. He has paid the price to bring you into his family forever. He has loved you until death and beyond.

The rich man from Bethlehem stirred under the stars. He sat up. Noticing his feet were uncovered he peered into the darkness. Someone was there by his feet. "Who are you?"

Her heart beat quickly. Her breath held. Here it came, the moment of truth.

"I am Ruth, your servant" (Ruth 3:9). Those were the easy words. Now came the difficult ones. "Spread out the skirt of your robe over your servant, for you are a family redeemer" (Ruth 3:9). The words sounded off the dark threshing floor. Could Ruth see his face under the stars? Did Boaz's mouth show hints of a smile or a grimace...joy or anger...redemption or rejection?

"May you be blessed by the Lord, my daughter!" (Ruth 3:10). Boaz's usual greeting carried greater meaning this night. "You have made your last act of kindness better than the first by not going to look for a young man, whether poor or rich" (Ruth 3:10). Boaz saw Ruth the same way she viewed him - a caring believer always ready to live their love. Then came the promise. "I will do everything that you are asking. Indeed, all the people at the city gate know that you are an honorable woman" (Ruth 3:11).

A kinsman redeemer dedicated himself to buying his relative's land, marrying this noble foreign woman and continuing the line of the Savior. All Ruth's nervousness, every concern that had so gripped her that night, melted away with the rising of the sun. Her answer came. Her salvation was at hand.

So is yours. Your long night waits will seem to last forever. At times, the good news you hoped for with all of your heart comes to fruition. Praise the Lord! Sometimes the answers you receive will concur with your worst fears. Your bridegroom doesn't abandon you in those moments either. Instead, he blesses you with the same comforting words he promised to a foreigner in Bethlehem, a promise meant for any and every believer who comes to him by faith in prayer:

Comfort for the Night

"So now, my daughter, do not be afraid. I will do everything that you are asking" (Ruth 3:11).

CHAPTER 14

Job's Dark Suffering

Job 4:12-17

Late one night, a woman was walking down into the blackness of her basement. The candle she held spread a dim light around the cellar room. Shadows danced everywhere as the flame moved in her hand. Then, piercing the silence of the night, she heard a most unnerving sound. As shivers shot up her spine the woman reached the middle of the cellar and held her candle up. The light revealed a horrifying sight—one she would never forget. The body of a dead man lay across her table. How did he die? Who brought him there? Where did the noise come from?

The answers didn't come quickly enough. A crack of thunder shook the room. The woman's eyes darted around the cellar. None of this seemed natural. She peered down at the dead man's face, still and cold.

His eyes opened. He stared right at her—seemingly right through her. Underneath lumbering noises he began to slowly sit up.

The woman dropped the candle, turned and ran as quickly as she could for the stairs. This now wide-awake monstrosity moved after her. His massive body pushed along his angry, dead eyes faster and faster. He was gaining on her.

She rushed up the stairs, looking back at the surging dead man. He was about to catch her. As she struggled through the door a crack of lightning brilliantly lit up house. The man's strong, cold, hand reached out to grab her. She couldn't move. She lifted her head to scream.

Then she woke up.

It had all been a dream. A thankful relief swept over the woman as she sat up in bed. But the dream stuck with her. Quickly rising out of bed, she frantically wrote down the nightmare on a nearby piece of paper.

The woman who dreamed the dream was Mary Shelley. You can read about her nightmare. She wrote it all down in a story entitled *Frankenstein*. Maybe you've heard of it. It has become one of the most famous novels ever written.

Nightmares can have strange effects on us. They draw us in to a sort of twilight world, catching us between the real and the fantastic, the stillness and the frenetic, and, in the case of Mary Shelley, the useless and the lucrative.

It was at precisely this twilight point that Eliphaz found himself. This friend of Job had had a nightmare real enough to frighten even Mary Shelley. In fact, the details sound rather similar to Shelley's monster.

In the middle of the night, Eliphaz had trouble falling asleep. A whisper swept through the room. Was he hearing things? Anxious thoughts ran through his mind. Terror and trembling seized him. That's when Eliphaz saw him. A tall, shadowy figure stood silently over him.

How would you react? Would you run screaming from the room? Many brave souls have melted at the sight of silent figures in the night. Those quiet, frightening moments have a way of ripping away any pretense of sanity and righteousness. The dark draws out our secret fears and hidden sins.

That's what happened to Eliphaz that night. The whisper came from the mysterious man standing before him. He had more to say. "Can a person be righteous before God? Can a man be pure before his Maker?" (Job 4:17).

Did this really happen? Was this a dream or a reality that Eliphaz experienced that night? Could he even tell the difference? Mary Shelley had difficulty telling the difference, too. Eventually, her monster became real enough to write about. Eliphaz's mystifying man in the darkness appeared real enough to relate to his friend Job.

But of all the frightening experiences displayed in the book of Job, the destruction of property, the loss of animals and—worst of all—the death of his children, Eliphaz's whisper remains the most dangerous. His words became poison for an already sick man.

After Job lost everything, including his health and the encouragement of his wife, he found himself desperately needing answers. Three of his friends came to give him answers. In this chapter, Eliphaz is the first to speak.

His advice is disastrous.

Eliphaz tells Job he is not righteous—that he deserves God's wrath as a sinner. But Job already knows this! Spooky stories aside, the most frightening aspect of the book of Job is the lack of gospel this repentant sinner hears. Job yearned for God's good news. But at this point, his friends only show him the law.

Do you have Eliphaz-like friends who speak this way to you? We all do. At points in our lives, in our darkest moments, when we yearn for the sound of forgiveness, many are too quick to bring more law. You tell the person you yelled at, "I'm sorry," only to hear in return "You always run your mouth—why is this any different!" When you needed to hear forgiveness you heard only judgment.

But there is an even more frightening prospect. Have you been the Eliphaz friend for others? We all have been. When the person who betrayed you made the difficult walk up to ask for your forgiveness, how did you respond? Sometimes we send our betrayer further down the path of despair. We refuse to offer forgiveness. We rationalize that we don't believe the person is ready to hear it—but the reality is that we are not ready to give it.

God's word doesn't tell us if Eliphaz knowingly kept God's gospel to himself or if he just didn't know any better. Either way, Job remained in despair. He would remain in despair for many more chapters. A darkness no light could pierce seemed to close in around him. Death appeared to stalk Job as quickly as Mary Shelley's monster.

Finally, Job arrived at the lowest point of desperation. After hearing from all of his friends multiple times he admitted his innermost feelings: "With all my heart I am weary of my life" (Job 10:1). Then, to the Lord himself, Job says the unthinkable, "Why, then, did you bring me out from the womb? I wish I had died" (Job 10:18).

Has the law sent you reeling to the black cellar of Job's soul? The devil buries you so deep under your own guilt that hope itself vanishes. That is when death starts to seem inviting. Maybe you can identify with Job's utter despair: "Nights of agony have been assigned to me. When I lie down, I think, 'How long before I get up?' But the night drags on, and I am filled with restlessness until dawn" (Job 7:3-4).

Don't give in to that hopelessness. Tell Eliphaz to shut up. The law that presses down so hard on you has already been pressed upon Jesus. The eternity of darkness and suffering that the devil tries so hard to get you to think is your future is actually Jesus' past.

To the repentant soul—to *you*—your Lord proclaims: "You are forgiven." These are not the whispers of a black figure hovering over a dark bedroom. Your Savior proclaimed your salvation from the cross. His gospel resounds through his empty tomb. Heaven is yours.

The Lord finally brought Job to that realization. He did not need to take his own life—nor should he have! Neither should you. Instead, God led the weak and weathered Job in the same way he cares for your distressed, despairing soul, taking you from the darkness of sin to the dawn of salvation.

Comfort for the Night

"In my own flesh I will see God. I myself will see him. My own eyes will see him, and not as a stranger" (Job 19:26-27).

CHAPTER 15

A Moonlit Meeting

1 Samuel 9:18-25

Melancholy struck Richard II, the King of England. In the Shakespearean play that bears his name it led him to pour out his heart in these memorable words:

> "Let us sit upon the ground
> And tell sad stories of the death of kings."[1]

History had taught the king to look over his shoulder. All sorts of plots and schemes had led to the death of kings. Would he be next? Richard II needed to peer into those dark truths before he could come to grips with reigning as king. After all, every king eventually dies. Few pass away because of old age.

Had the prophet Samuel peered into that same darkness that Richard II contemplated? Considering the circumstances, he would have certainly shared in Richard's melancholy. Not since Moses had God's people so quickly turned on a leader. After years and years of faithful service, having led Israel from godless idolatry to faithful obedience, Samuel now stood as a relic from a bygone era. His sons were wicked. No one wanted them to lead. Besides all this, prophet-leaders were a thing of the past. Kingdoms didn't operate that way anymore.

Israel wanted a king. So, they summoned the prophet one last time. Ready to hand him a gold watch and an honorable retirement,

---

[1] Edited by W. G. Clark, *Richard II* (Oxford: Oxford Press, 1876), 45.

Israel's elders gathered to see their old leader ride off quietly into the sunset.

How do you react when the people you have served for so long want to replace you? Offense might be the first emotion that arrives. Anger quickly follows. Eventually, melancholy arrives, threatening never to leave.

"Let us sit upon the ground
And tell sad stories of the death of kings."

Samuel was ready to give his Richard II speech. He shared with his people a stern warning about the hardships a king brings (much like Moses had done hundreds of years earlier). Nobody listened. They had made up their minds.

The sad story of the kings of Israel begins at this point. Samuel brings the people's request to the Lord. The Lord promises to bless his people with a king. Just like that, the Lord joined the retirement song of the people for the old prophet. His years of faithful service were coming to a close.

First he had to anoint his replacement.

It is always strange to train your replacement. Sinful nature wants nothing to do with the man. The devil tempts you to inject a poison pill into the instruction to make your work look better by comparison. The world encourages, even expects, this type of retribution. Vengeance can be a powerful tool, especially when it is placed in the hand of an individual who has felt wronged. Discussions in office cubicles can feel just as perilous as whispers in the halls of kings.

At that very moment, the man God selected to be the first king of Israel was lost. He searched the fields looking for his missing donkeys. That's when he found the prophet Samuel. What did Samuel think when he first saw Saul? Did jaded thoughts lead him to become skeptical of this Benjaminite? Once they start talking, Saul himself sounded skeptical of his own kingly prospects. "I am just a Benjaminite from the smallest of the tribes of Israel. And my family is the least important of all the families in the tribe of Benjamin" (1 Sam 9:21).

But similar to the approach of the Lord, these details did not matter to Samuel. In a meal already prepared, he honored Saul with the choice cut of meat. Then followed one of the most important nights for either leader. Samuel took Saul to the top of the roof and they talked.

We have no written record of their discussions. If we could only be a fly on that roof! Did Samuel recount the Lord's instruction concerning kings from Deuteronomy 17? Did the two just get to know each other? Perhaps they sat down and discussed the sad stories about the death of kings.

Over the next couple centuries, many kings would reign over Israel. While very few of them were murdered or executed, so many of them died spiritually. In fact, the history of God's Old Testament kings is a veritable "what not to do" for leaders.

It all started with Saul.

What would you have said to the young man upon the roof? Would your words sound like the incessant ramblings of an old codger, angry at your replacement and vindictive toward the world? Would you genuinely try to help the poor soul step into a role he never thought he would hold? Would you just stay silent?

For all of his anger and hurt, Samuel does genuinely help Saul. He patiently instructs him. He prepares God's chosen man to become Israel's first king.

Saul's reign would not go well. He would become the first in a long list of spiritually dead kings. Sadly, Samuel would remain around long enough to see it all happen. But on that night, on the eve of Saul's kingly anointing, the prophet gently preached.

It takes patience to instruct someone who is replacing you. In those moments, melancholy arrives as the unwanted guest. Sometimes he brings despair with him, especially when it seems as though the world no longer has need of you. *Am I still wanted?*

Jesus filled his ministry on earth with moments like this. He witnessed rejection. He watched even his closest friends abandon him when he needed them most. He felt the entire world turn against him. He even experienced his own Father sentence him with eternal punishment.

No person has ever felt such extreme rejection and abandonment. Jesus willingly accepted the entire ordeal for you. He knows your vindictiveness. He has seen your thoughts of anger and despair. He has watched as you poisoned your replacement with poor instruction. He took your punishment for each and every one of those sins.

In fact, he has done even more than that. His Holy Spirit has worked through the word and the waters of baptism to anoint you.

He made you his, to live and serve in his kingdom. All this he accomplished for you so that he could bring you to the top of the roof. He knows your nights have been long. He understands what you are up against. He foresees every disaster coming your way. On this rooftop he reminds you in his word that he has all of these difficulties under control.

Do you see what Jesus is doing? He is training you to be his replacement. No, you are not going to be the Savior of the world—he has already won salvation for everyone. He is sending you out at his ambassador. He is equipping you to serve, the way he served you. Go into all the world. Sit and tell the sad story of the death of the King. Then share the truth of his glorious resurrection.

Eventually, the prophet and the king came down off the roof. Samuel anointed Saul. In his coronation speech, Samuel spoke words that transcended the moment. His words, beautiful in their simplicity, are meant for you, too…

Comfort for the Night

"God is with you" (1 Sam 10:7).

CHAPTER 16

A Night for Murder

1 Samuel 26

Two men silently stood over the King of Israel. He was fast asleep, completely unaware of their presence in his tent. The minds of the two intruders raced. Looking around the royal tent they saw a water jug and a spear. The spear stuck in the ground right beside the king's head.

One of the men whispered with a determined voice, "God has delivered your enemy into your hand today" (1 Sam 26:8). His partner could not disagree. There slept King Saul, the first king of Israel, surrounded by an entire camp of soldiers who were also fast asleep. The only way an entire military encampment could sleep so soundly through the night was if God put them all to sleep. From the guards on the perimeter to the king in the middle, not a man moved.

Abishai spoke up again, this time with even more determination, "Please let me strike him and pin him to the ground with my spear. One blow! That's all I'll need! I won't need to strike him a second time" (1 Sam 26:8).

Now that was an interesting prospect. Maybe Abishai had a point. Saul had been hunting them down with unrelenting vigor for months—or perhaps even years. He had pursued David from his own house to the priestly town of Nob. Saul had raised the Israelite army to hunt down David and his men through Philistia and a cave called Adullam and a place named Mizpah in Moab. Throughout this murderous chase Saul massacred priests and drove out families. He even threatened the lives of his own children when they sided with David.

Now, under a veil of darkness the tables had turned. No more running. No more murdering of innocents. It could all end with

Abishai's spear pinning Saul to the ground forever. Israel's first anointed king, Saul, would give way to Israel's second anointed king, David. This shepherd boy turned armor-bearer already held the hearts of the people in his hand. Now it seemed as though the Lord himself had orchestrated the coup.

Maybe Abishai was on to something.

What happens when the prey becomes the predator? Videos of the animal kingdom can reveal just how strange it can look. Rabbits turn on venomous snakes in order to save their bundle of bunnies. Along South Africa's Sabie River a herd of Cape buffalo march together against a pride of lions, pushing the predators away as if they were nothing but groundhogs.

Interestingly enough, each of these instances end when the prey-turned-predator is no longer in danger. Sometimes they actually kill their predator. Other times they simply get away. In the end, survival remains their key motivator.

What about you? What if you stepped into the tent of your unsuspecting enemy? How would you treat him? What would you do to her? Humans are different from animals in a variety of ways. One of those differences is when the hunted becomes the hunter. Survival isn't always the sole motivating factor. Usually revenge grabs that most important seat.

Now I know what you're thinking. *I'm not the vengeful type. I'd never kill another soul!* Maybe not. But maybe the Lord simply never gave you the opportunity. As humans we struggle with sin both internally and externally. We are all capable of committing crimes we dare not think about.

So, did you put a face to that sleeping soul you are standing over in the tent? What put him there? What did she say that betrayed your trust and ruined your life? Perhaps the person hunted you down to destroy you out of jealousy, like Saul was doing with David. Your sister turned on you, like she always does. Your pastor let you down when you needed him most. Someone, a soul whose name you don't even know, threatened you.

Now you stand over him. You have her in your grasp. What do you really want to say? What would you really do? Go on, be honest. It's just you and me.

Maybe…just maybe…you would do something you would later regret. You would shout the person into oblivion—making her think twice about ever crossing you again. You would pummel him so hard that his own mother wouldn't recognize him. Or, most devious of all, you would slowly, methodically, ruin their life by taking away the possessions and people they held most dear. Drip by drip you would watch their heart bleed out until their very soul dried up in agony.

I know these are difficult thoughts to admit. But they have to be. If you are going to enter this text honestly then you have to walk into the tent with Abishai. You need to listen to his whispers in the night, understanding you have said those words, too. "One blow! That's all I'll need!"

Abishai's most dangerous words sound almost too sweet, don't they? "God has delivered your enemy into your hand today" (1 Sam 26:8). Sinful nature loves to appeal to our sense of self-righteousness, as though God understands our plight enough to overlook every one of his commandments and allow us to enact revenge. *Come on, God, just this once.*

Once is all it takes. Abishai said so. "I won't need to strike him a second time" (1 Sam 26:8).

Enter this chapter of Scripture honestly, the same way you enter God's house. Walk in like Abishai, carrying every vengeful thought and angry outburst to your Lord in confession. Those are difficult admonitions: thoughts of murder, words of destruction, acts of reprisal.

Then hear David's calm but confident whisper in return. "Do not destroy him, for who can stretch out his hand against the Lord's anointed and be guiltless?" (1 Sam 26:9). Those words guide the confession we make to the Lord at the beginning of worship. We are not guiltless. Countless victims lay in the streets of our murderous thoughts.

No Davidic voice spoke up when the Anointed One stood among the guilty in Jerusalem. Instead, the Jewish leaders stretched out their hands to strike the Christ, the Anointed One. They thought they were guiltless. They gave the same excuses Abishai made a millennium earlier. Maybe God had delivered Jesus into their hands in order to allow them to enact their vengeance.

They had it half right.

God did indeed deliver himself into their hands, but not because they were guiltless. He was apprehended precisely because they were guilty—because we *all* were guilty. Then came David's other pronouncement, "As the Lord lives, the Lord will strike him, or his day will come and he will die, or he will go down into battle and be swept away" (1 Sam 26:10). That day came quickly for Saul. At a mountain called Gilboa, Israel's first king was wounded. He killed himself rather than allow his enemy to apprehend him.

Christ did no such thing. He suffered for the murderous thoughts, words and actions of his enemies. The one who could have been the ultimate, omnipotent predator willingly became the weakest of prey. And God died.

And then God rose again. And that empty tomb continues to echo a pronouncement that now rings out in churches throughout the world—straight to you: "Your sins are forgiven."

That forgiveness led David to pick up Saul's spear and leave the royal tent. Neither David nor Saul knew it, but their ensuing conversation would be their last. Saul repented. And David spoke a beautiful final gospel proclamation...perhaps the final one Saul would ever hear. "Just as your life was precious in my eyes today, so let my life be precious in the Lord's eyes" (1 Sam 26:24).

Your enemy's life is precious in your Lord's sight. Don't spend tonight plotting your revenge. Spend your evening praying for him, for her, for them by name. Let the words of a king who intimately knows your struggle help you...

Comfort for the Night

"By day the Lord commands his mercy, and at night his song is with me—a prayer to the God of my life" (Ps 42:8).

CHAPTER 17

Sins of the Father

2 Samuel 12:14-17

"Children are the most delightful pledges of a loving marriage."[1] Martin Luther once penned those happy words to a friend of his. We don't know when he wrote the letter, but we can readily imagine him observing his own delightful children at the time. The Lord had blessed Martin and his wife Katharina with six children, although their first daughter died in infancy. But of their three sons and three daughters, Luther had a special place in his heart for young Magdalene. He called her *Sweet Lenchen*, which was both a nickname and a loving term of endearment that meant "beautiful."

Then, in 1542, Luther's heart broke. His now thirteen year-old daughter, Magdalene, had been sick for quite some time. It was becoming apparent that she would not recover. On perhaps the saddest day of Luther's life, he entered Magdalene's room. Glancing to the wall he noticed again her portrait, painted by the talented Lucus Cranach. Looking to the bed he saw the deep eyes of his sweet Lenchen looking back at him. Luther then said the words no father would ever want to share with his daughter, "My little Magdalena, my little girl, soon you will not be with me."[2]

As life began to escape her, the father asked his daughter one final question: "Magdalene, my dear little daughter, would you like to

---

[1] Ewald M. Plass, *What Luther Says* (St. Louis: Concordia Publishing House, 1959), 137.

[2] Scott H. Hendrix, *Martin Luther: A Very Short Introduction* (New York: Oxford University Press, 2010), 76.

stay here with your father, or would you willingly go to your Father yonder?" Softly she answered, "Dear father, as God wants."[3]

Moments later Magdalene died.

Luther and his wife greatly struggled with the loss of their Magdalene. Their crying and grieving were so great that it was as if a piece of them had died that day as well. Luther later admitted to a friend, "The words and the movements of the living and dying daughter remain deeply engraved in our hearts."[4]

It isn't supposed to happen that way. Fathers and mothers are not meant to outlive their children. When death does rush in through the doors of a loving home, it leaves an empty sadness for the living to feel the rest of their lives.

Have you watched over the bed of your sick child, keeping guard while she sleeps? "Helpless" only begins to describe your heart as you sit, unable to help her. Frustration pours out next. Guilt soon follows. If only you could trade places with your little one—you would make the switch in an instant! I know your love for your child, I have that same love for my children. I would want to take their ailment on myself forever if it would save them.

Martin Luther deeply understood those emotions. So did King David. While Luther and his family watched their daughter suffer and die as an overall result of sin and a sinful world, David watched helplessly as his infant son lay dying because of his own sin.

The king had rebelled against the Lord. The wreckage of David's sins left dead and dying souls littered behind him. Unable to save his own child, David does what he often did in times of crisis. He wrote a psalm.

"Against you, you only, have I sinned, and I have done this evil in your eyes" (Ps 51:4). This would not just be any psalm. David's turmoil and guilt over his own sins would permeate these words and melodies more than any other piece of music he wrote. Pure, heart-wrenching admonition rips away the last shreds of veneer the king once possessed. Black ash replaces his golden crown. Sackcloth becomes his new robe.

---

[3] Weimar Ausgabe Tischreden: WATR, 5497, 5498, 5499. Accessed at https://archive.org/stream/werketischreden10205luthuoft#page/n13/mode/2up on 10-12-2020.

[4] Hendrix, 77.

Looking upon his sick boy, David recalls the sin that accompanied his own birth. "Certainly, I was guilty when I was born. I was sinful when my mother conceived me" (Ps 51:5). For a king like David his sins bore an extra cost. Others always seemed to bear the brunt of his sins.

The Judge carrying out this discipline on the House of David was none other than the Lord himself. That must have hurt David the most. His son was dying because of his own sins of adultery, falsehood and murder, yet it was the Lord who had to carry out the sentence.

Please understand that this punishment in 2 Samuel 12 was extraordinary. The Lord does not strike your child with an illness, or even death, because you committed some outlandishly heinous sin. Like David, you have been sinful from birth. You struggle with sin every day. I only share this with you because I am sinful, too. You and I both need to remember that.

When the Lord punishes people in the Bible for specific sins he is always very careful to explain everything. David knew exactly what was happening because the prophet Nathan had shared God's intentions with him. By the grace of God, Israel's king repented of his sins. "Against you, you only, have I sinned, and I have done this evil in your eyes" (Ps 51:4).

But the consequences remained. "Because by this deed you have treated the Lord with utter contempt, the child that is born to you shall surely die" (2 Sam 12:14). David did everything he could to plead for the Lord's mercy. Like any father at the deathbed of his child, like any mother pleading with the Lord to take away the illness from a baby, David "spent the night lying on the ground" (2 Sam 12:16).

But God wants you to know that your child isn't sick because of anything you did. Your baby did not die because you are an extra-awful sinner. Death is a result of the sin we are born with. Death comes to everybody.

It was never meant to be that way. When God created his perfect world, death was nowhere to be found. But when sin entered into our world death followed. Despite what we hear from people at funerals, death is not natural. Death was never meant to exist.

But death does exist. A powerful tyrant, death mercilessly swings his sickle cutting down old and young alike. And how are we to feel about that? You know the progression of emotions by now: helplessness, frustration, guilt.

But God doesn't witness our grief as an outside observer. He knows what it is like to lose a child. Like David, God the Father knew death was coming for his Son. He saw it from eternity. And he refused to do anything to stop it. God's love for you prevented him from helping his Son avoid death. All the Father could do was remove himself and allow Jesus to suffer the eternity of hell for every sinful father and mother, child and infant.

The Son of God died.

Then the Son of God came back to life. He really did wash away sin. He really did defeat our enemy the devil. He really did open heaven for you. And he really did defeat death.

Yes, even death.

Everyone understood David's fatherly grief by the bed of his dying infant son. Only after his son died did his household become offended by his actions. In their defense, it probably seemed strange to watch the weeping king dry his tears, get changed and worship in the house of the Lord. Their surprise finally led them to ask their king about his actions.

David opened his heart to them. "While the child was alive, I fasted and wept because I said, 'Who knows? Will the Lord be gracious to me and let my child live?'" (2 Sam 12:22). But the child had died. God's will was done. And David looked beyond the grave. "Am I able to return him to life again? I will go to him, but he will not return to me" (2 Sam 12:23).

Have you lost a little one? Was your son or daughter, grandson or granddaughter taken from you? Look at their baptism with the confidence. It won them into God's family and clothed them for their heavenly home. Have you lost a child before baptism was possible? Have you wondered if it doomed your unborn infant? God understands her circumstance better than you or I. Place that child into the loving arms of your loving Father. Remember, he knows what it is like to lose a son. He is here with you in his word now to point you to the resurrection to which King David looked ahead.

Martin Luther looked ahead to that glorious resurrection as well. As he wrote his friend about his emotional struggle at the death of his beloved daughter, Magdalena, Luther looked to the same resurrection

David did. By faith he remembered his Savior who loves children… *his* children. And with tears of both sadness and joy streaming down Luther's face, he ended his letter thinking of his daughter's last moments on earth. In that dark room, at that moment of death, Magdalena's God-given faith shown most brightly.

As always, Luther summarized the situation perfectly: "God grant me and all my loved ones and all our friends such a death—or rather such a life."[5]

Comfort for the Night

"Do not cast me from your presence. Do not take your Holy Spirit from me. Restore to me the joy of your salvation. Sustain me with a willing spirit" (Ps 51:11-12).

---

[5] Hendrix, 77.

CHAPTER 18

Night Watch

1 Chronicles 9:23-27

They heard Nazi soldiers shouting. Blasts from German cannons exploded on the mountain. British sirens sounded in the night. The rock of Gibraltar, the mountain guarding the Atlantic from the Mediterranean was witnessing her worst day. All throughout the miles of tunnels dug beneath her hard exterior, men scurried to find their positions. Cannons housed in the caverns peeked out through small openings in the rock. Their booming explosions echoed through the tunnels of stone.

It was too late. Thousands of Nazi soldiers invaded the tunnels like enemy ants. British officers frantically grabbed their important papers. Only some escaped. Many more died protecting the mountain fortress of Gibraltar.

For six men, however, the scene looked quite different. While other soldiers fired cannons and fought the Nazis in hand-to-hand combat, these six soldiers quickly hid away in a secret cave in the mountain. These men, consisting of an executive officer, two doctors and three wireless radio operators caved in the entrance to their own tunnel. They trapped themselves in the deep recesses of Gibraltar, surrounded by Nazis. There was no way out.

Their British leaders had prepared them for this possibility. At the end of those hidden rooms they had cut a hole through which these six soldiers could view the movements of the enemy. Using their wireless radio, powered by a stationary bicycle, they were to report back to British intelligence everything they saw. The hope was that these men would only be trapped behind the rock, surrounded by Nazis for no more than a year. If the situation became dire, they were to prepare for a seven year stay.

This is the part where I have to tell you that none of this actually happened. Only the plan and the provisions existed for this harrowing sacrifice. British intelligence did indeed select half a dozen soldiers on Gibraltar for this ominous task. Their training for this mission would have looked and sounded an awful lot like what you just read. But it never happened.

In the decades following World War II, rumors bounced around about this secret fallback mission. The idea of this six-man assignment beneath the rock of Gibraltar drew people in. It aroused imaginations. Many wondered what it would have been like to live in a sealed cave, surrounded by Nazis, secretly marking out enemy movements. What would happen when tempers flared in their cramped confines? Would years of sacrifice to duty eventually take its toll on the men? Why has this movie not been written?

Your imagination can become reality, if you are able to get to those old British fortifications. To this day you can visit the secret, carved out cave on Gibraltar. Guests are encouraged to imagine themselves operating in the once-sealed environs as they look out at the bay through the small slit in the rock. The place still goes by the ominous name it was called during the war: The Stay Behind Room.

No such room existed in Old Testament Israel. Yet the Lord tasked a group of men to do the work of stay-behind British soldiers. All the way back when the house of the Lord was still a tent, four Levites were selected to stay behind during the night and guard the tabernacle.

The service probably did not involve hand-to-hand combat. I doubt any Nazis ever attempted an invasion of the premises. And yet, the task was meant to be an honor. To guard the house of the Lord—who could ask for a higher post?

The Sons of Korah, those Old Testament psalm writers, described these very men standing at attention to the entrance of the temple when they wrote Psalm 84. "I would rather wait at the doorway of the house of my God than dwell in the tents of the wicked" (Ps 84:10).

It all sounds so romantic—the stalwart guard standing over the temple through sun and rain, day and night. But was it really? These guards must have had moments when they did need to be ready for hand-to-hand combat. They needed to protect the temple from ene-mies, or even those struggling with mental illness looking to wander inside. Yes, they guarded the temple, but they must have also had to protect sinful people from the temple. One wrong move and death could swallow them up. It had happened before—to the very sons of the first high priest, Aaron.

But guard duty doesn't always feel like an honor. There must have been moments when the night grew long and the guards' eyes grew heavy. Parades and festivities took place elsewhere. Family meals on important days like the Passover could not draw these men away from their duty. And there are moments when I wonder—and maybe you do too—when their task would have been too much for them. Were there moments when they felt trapped behind the rock walls of their mission…like the last six soldiers on Gibraltar?

Do you have a fortress of solitude? Is there an escape you yearn for when this world gets too grim? Sometimes being a Christian feels like standing alone in the dark, guarding something not too many people care about anymore. In your moments of despair, perhaps you even feel trapped by a world of enemies. Is anyone coming to relieve you of your position…even for a moment?

The night drags on and so do your struggles. You guard your faith, but so many want to argue it out of you. You want to live by the Truth, but laziness and fear fester within. You desire to be that mis-sionary that speaks out about the importance of God's Word to your neighbors, but then you keep silent so that you can keep the peace.

Standing guard is a difficult task…perhaps one of the most dif-ficult tasks. Soldiers must simultaneously stand at attention and not harm. Is such a calling even possible? It becomes so difficult for us to strike that balance in our own lives. God tells you to stand on his Word, always being ready to live it and share it—even in the darkness of this world. But then your eyes grow heavy. You waver.

God sends you out as his ambassador, to speak his truth in love. But sometimes you have bludgeoned others with God's Word, expect-ing immediate results—or no results. You and I have been the guard equipped with God's Word, picking a fight with those who walk by.

Both extremes threaten a guard in the night. And the nights seem to grow longer every year. Weakness eats away at us. Loneliness remains our lot in this life.

Long after guards left the temple a different type of soldier entered Jerusalem. He had not come with any weapons. No heavily equipped entourage followed. He was all alone—the last lonely guard of the night.

The world hated him for that. They antagonized him. They tried to draw anger and vengeance out of him with slaps and spitting and scourging. They knew that if they could get this guard to balk, he would be nothing more than one of them.

But Jesus wasn't one of them. Yes, he had become a human—he had taken on flesh. But no sin resided in him. Your perfect Savior opposed the darkness that surrounded him. He didn't give in. Instead, he took it upon himself—hell and all. The perfect guard turned day into night as he hung on a cross. He willingly died at his post to save you from an eternity of darkness.

He was buried behind a sealed rock. That was part of his mission, too. But this Gibraltar-like tomb would not house him for years and years. Only days.

A beautiful Easter morning finally arrived. The stone rolled away. The mission was complete. Forever.

Now this guard who gave his life for you assigns you as a guard of his Word. It won't be easy. He has always been up front about that. Darkness will surround you at times. Enemies will try to draw you out into vengeance. Loneliness will come.

But you are not alone. Like the temple guards of old, hold on to those psalms sung around you—psalms singing your sure and certain hope. "Come, bless the Lord, all you servants of the Lord, who stand in the house of the Lord at night" (Ps 134:1).

Your strength for this post doesn't come from inside yourself. It comes from your Lord. Look to him every day…and every night.

Comfort for the Night

"How blessed is everyone whose strength is found in you" (Ps 84:5).

CHAPTER 19

An Eve of Bad News

1 Chronicles 17:1-15

How do you preface bad news? Maybe you tell the person to sit down first—just in case they faint from the message. Perhaps you share some happy news to prepare their hearts for what is coming next. Maybe you just keep the bad news to yourself.

The approach to sharing bad news has changed over the years. A century ago, when doctors discovered that a child had cancer, they simply chose to tell the child she would soon get better. The heart wrenching truth seemed too awful to bear, especially for little children. As recently as the 1960s, doctors thought it best that they not tell their patients when diseases like cancer threatened their life.[1]

Today in America, full-disclosure remains the preferred approach. Tough as it can be, doctors share their complete prognosis with the family. Understandably, these conversations can be the most difficult. Maybe that is why it took so many years for doctors to start having them.

Perhaps you haven't been on either side of bad news in a doctor's office. But have you ever received an "untitled" email from someone you know? Those can be the worst! Either they are a quick little message that didn't need a title in the subject box, or they are such an emotional, scathing rebuke that no title could possibly define them.

---

[1] Fallowfield LJ, Jenkins VA, Beveridge HA. "Truth May Hurt but Deceit Hurts More: Communication in Palliative Care." *Palliative medicine* Vol. 16,4 (2002): 297-303.

My heart flutters a little each time I see an "untitled" email. Maybe you know the feeling.

Bad news remains so difficult to hear. Yet God is pretty straightforward when he talks about receiving bad news. "An ear that listens to a life-giving warning will find a home among the wise" (Prov 15:31). Sticking your head in the sand does not make bad news vanish.

So, what was the prophet Nathan to do? In 1 Chronicles 17, King David proposed a beautiful building project for the Lord. Whenever he looked out at the tent-like tabernacle of the Lord from his own mansion David felt guilty. To correct the problem, David planned to build a house befitting the Lord and his Ark of the Covenant. In the moment, Nathan responded the way any prophet would want to respond: "Do everything that is in your heart, because God is with you" (1 Chr 17:2).

It was a mistake. Nathan was too quick in his response. He thought it was a good idea, but he never actually asked the Lord.

The following night must have been a long one for the prophet. As he often does, Lord shares the bad news first. "This is what the Lord says. You will not be the one to build a house for me to live in" (1 Chr 17:4). Those initial words must have hit Nathan like a ton of bricks. He had shared his personal "go-ahead" with David, but that was not the response from the Lord. Now, during the night, Nathan has to hear "what *the Lord* says" (1 Chr 17:4).

We all know how Nathan feels. There are moments when we are too quick to share our personal approval with someone before actually seeing what the Lord has to say on the subject. When your son wants to live with his girlfriend before they get married, you might be tempted to respond quickly: "I wouldn't do it that way, but who am I to get in the way of your happiness." What God actually says sounds like bad news. "Indeed, this is God's will: that you be sanctified, namely, that you keep yourselves away from sexual immorality" (1 Thess 4:3).

During that long night, Nathan had to come to grips with the fact that he would have to say "No" to his king the next morning. Walking back yesterday's exuberance would be humiliating enough. How would David respond to no longer being the Lord's temple-building king?

Of course, it wasn't all bad news. The Lord armed Nathan with the greatest news any king could hear. This was the type of information that would sustain Nathan through his long evening. This good news was greater than any temple project.

The next day the prophet Nathan shared the word of the Lord— all of it. David would not be the king to build the house of the Lord. Neither 2 Samuel 7 nor 1 Chronicles 17 share David's initial response to this bad news. He might have frowned, squirming on his throne with initial discontentment.

But then came the good news of the Lord. David would not build a house for the Lord. Instead, the Lord would build a house for King David. This house would not be made of stone and wood. Gold would not need to adorn these walls. God would establish the household of David forever.

"Good news from a distant country is like cold water for a weary soul" (Prov 25:25). Solomon, a son of David, wrote those words. He knew what he was talking about. He knew that this promise to establish his father's household went beyond him. The "seed" God would raise up from the line of David would be the Son of God.

Jesus fulfilled this promise. He came as great David's greater Son. One of the reasons Jesus came was to share news—both good and bad. Think of all the bad news Jesus shared during his ministry. He warned of false teachers who resembled wolves in sheep's clothing (Matt 7:15). He prophesied the signs that would usher in the destruction of Jerusalem (Luke 21:20). He predicted his own rejection, capture and crucifixion (Mark 8:31).

The news didn't get any better for his disciples. Jesus told them that they would abandon him (Matt 26:31). He shared that one day they would be handed over to the authorities of this world (Luke 21:12). He informed them that they would be betrayed by family members closest to them and be put to death (Luke 21:16).

Then came the good news. Jesus would arm his followers with his word when the wolves would come. He would protect his people even in the midst of destruction. He would forgive his disciples for abandoning him. He would stand with his people when they stood before rulers. And Jesus promised that he would never betray his people, even when the world betrays them. That includes you.

Then Jesus proved it. He proved it by fulfilling his own prophecy. He allowed himself to be betrayed and apprehended and crucified. He took the worst news of all, the hell that should have been ours, and he had it thrust upon himself. He went through all that suffering—even death itself—to assure you of the greatest news you could ever hear. Your sins are forgiven. Heaven is yours.

The prophet Nathan was too quick to share his own version of the good news. But God's news was far better, even if it contained truths that David didn't want to hear. In the end, the prophet Nathan corrected himself. Did you catch it? The final words of this portion of God's word tell us that "Nathan told David all the words that had been revealed in this vision" (1 Chr 17:15). There is no greater epitaph describing a prophet of the Lord than that.

This is the very word God equips you to share. There will be truths that others don't want to hear. Don't gloss over them. Don't hide them. Share them boldly and lovingly.

Then share God's gospel news with just that same boldness and love that your Savior used when he shared it with you.

Comfort for the Night

"The righteous will be remembered forever. He will not fear bad news. His heart is steadfast, trusting in the Lord" (Ps 112:7-8).

CHAPTER 20

Siege Shadows

2 Kings 6:8-23

The Polish military had never quite seen someone like Wojtek. As armies collided into each other during World War II, Wojtek seemed to come into the Polish army from out of nowhere. Unlike most others in the military in those dark days, Wojtek sometimes acted as though a war wasn't even going on.

Wojtek loved practical jokes. When the men swam in the nearby river, he would swim under the water and pop up right in front of people, scaring them half to death. He loved to snatch all the men's underwear as they dried on the line. No one seemed to get out of sorts about all his joking around. They just simply said, "Oh, Wojtek."

He loved to walk the fine line between being amazingly popular and completely annoying. Sometimes, when everyone was sleeping in their tents, he would get up - almost franticly - and run all over everyone and wake them up. But he didn't just run. Wojtek would stand and fight, too. He was also an incredible boxer. Nobody could beat him.

But there was one other strange characteristic of Wojtek. During the night he would sneak into the shower and use up all the rationed water. It annoyed everybody to no end. Eventually, however, everyone would get past the inconvenience.

But on one fateful night, Wojtek's late-night hijinks saved the entire battalion.

One dark night, Wojtek once again snuck out to take one of his midnight showers—perhaps cooling down in the desert heat of Iraq. While he was there, he found an Arab spy hiding. When the man saw

Wojtek he was so surprised that he screamed. The spy was captured and the Polish position remained a secret to the enemy.

Sometimes, things are not always what they seem. Someone like Wojtek might annoy the soldiers of the Polish army with his practical joking and late-night antics, but when their lives were on the line, he saved them. World War II is filled with heroic stories like that—seemingly miraculous events that people never saw coming.

Scripture is filled with miraculous events, too—conditions that were not as they seemed.

Behind the walls of a town called Dothan, disaster appeared imminent. Under the cover of darkness, the Aramean army mounted their offensive against the prophet Elisha's town. Elisha's servant woke up to the sight no Middle Eastern citizen would ever want to see. Chariots and horses, soldiers and weapons surrounded the town. A siege now cornered every soul in town.

It was all too much for Elisha's servant. "Oh, my lord, what shall we do?" (2 Kgs 6:15). There was no Wojtek there to haunt the showers of the enemy and discover their plans. In fact, no heroes could be found. The situation appeared hopeless.

"Oh, my lord, what shall we do?"

Long anxious nights have a way of leading us to that question. Have you asked it lately? "Oh, my *Lord*, what shall we do?" Your relationships are in shambles. Your children are angry with you, refusing to listen to you. Your soul breaks over the hardships that surround you.

Enemies place you under siege as well. You see your neighbors disagreeing with the church you attend and the beliefs you hold. You witness your country moving ever further away from God's expectations laid out in his word. You watch as the family members you love take less of an interest in God and his word.

"Oh, my Lord, what shall we do?"

What we see can blind us from what is unseen. The devil and his evil angels attempt to surround us physically and spiritually. Your sinful nature tries every day to pull you down into the depths of despair and doubt. A world of enemies sees you as a threat to their lives of blissful ignorance.

"Oh, my Lord, what shall we do?"

But you are not doomed to blindness forever. You need to see everything, especially as the devil's darkness descends. Watch as Elisha opens your eyes to everything that matters.

"O Lord, open his eyes so that he can see" (2 Kgs 6:17).

All at once, chariots and soldiers come into view. An army larger than any other on earth stands behind you and around you. That's what happened at Dothan. "The Lord opened the servant's eyes, and he saw that the hills were full of horses and chariots of fire, all around Elisha" (2 Kgs 6:17).

The Aramean army was defeated and they didn't even know it yet. The besiegers were under siege. God's people stood protected by their Almighty and his holy hosts.

When Jesus came to earth, everything looked wrong. Jesus appeared to be just like any other man. He hung out with cast-offs. He didn't seem in control at all.

That looked especially true during the Passion history of our Lord. While Jesus prayed during his long night in Gethsemane, one of his disciples, Judas Iscariot, arrived with a mob. They were about to arrest Jesus under the cover of night. No one would see what they were doing. Darkness would make the perfect cover.

Like he did in Dothan, the Lord himself revealed the real situation. "Every day I was with you in the temple courts, and you did not lay a hand on me. But this is your hour—when darkness reigns" (Luke 22:53).

The Lord of Light willingly walked through that darkness to the cross. And now he shows you the cross for what it really is. It wasn't a defeat of God - it was his victory. It wasn't the end of Christianity, it was her beginning. It wasn't hopeless - it gives us our sure and certain hope!

"When we were overwhelmed by sins, you forgave our transgressions" (Ps 65:3).

The Holy Spirit has blessed you with that same sight of faith Elisha had on the walls of that city. He enables you to see this world for what it really is—to see your Lord for who he really is.

Things aren't always what they seem. The world looks like it is falling apart—but look again and see that God preserves it. Christianity appears to lose more followers every year—but look again and see how God strengthens his people with his Word.

That Polish army looked like they had a rabble-rouser in their midst. Wojtek woke them up at night. His nighttime showers used up all their water. He played his practical jokes that could be more than just annoying.

But look again. Wojtek isn't the man you think he is. In fact, Wojtek wasn't a man at all. Wojtek was a *bear*. That's right…an actual bear that the Polish army found and kept. Wojtek the bear played those jokes. He boxed. He took those showers. And yes, Wojtek the bear saved that battalion.

Things aren't always what they seem. Your life may not look successful now. Joy may be a distant memory. Long nights and lonely days may seem like your future forever. They are not. Christ won the victory over your every enemy. Your sadness will end. Struggle will cease—perhaps not in this life, but certainly in the one to come. Jesus promises that. Remember, he is the one who spoke through the prophet Elisha to a servant who needed to see clearly. He promises those words to you, too…

Comfort for the Night

"Don't be afraid, for those who are with us are more than those who are with them" (2 Kgs 6:16).

Chapter 21

The Black Belly

Jonah 2

Moving feet kicked up dust everywhere along the streets. Animals noisily changed hands while loud mouths bartered over prices. Children ran across the road, chasing one another with the carefree joy that comes from having no responsibilities. Rickety wagon wheels creaked along. Tempers flared. Women laughed with one another. Every city Augustine had ever traveled to within his Roman Empire revealed scenes like these.

This wasn't so much a busy day as it was a normal day. If you take the time to read through Augustine's numerous writings—and I strongly encourage you to do so—you get the feeling he quickly grew tired of the sights and sounds of busy market-places. Augustine loved his fellow Romans. He just couldn't always stand all the noise and hassle.

Maybe it all reminded him of his former life. Have you heard how Augustine spent his youth? He certainly doesn't hide anything in his autobiographical book *Confessions*. In fact, he admits to a time when he loved to sin. Lying, theft, sexual exploits—Augustine admitted to it all. Sometimes finding a crowd in which to hide, or a group from which to curry favor, makes these sins evermore inviting.

But later, as a pastor looking to meditate on God's Word, Augustine needed an escape from the noise and temptation. He knew others did as well. In a sermon, he shared this advice:

"Let us leave a little room for reflection in our lives. Let us leave room for periods of silence. Let us enter into ourselves; let us leave behind all noise and confusion. Let us look within ourselves and see whether there is some delightful hidden place in our consciousness where we can be free of noise and argument, where we need not be carrying on our disputes and planning to have our own stubborn way. Let us hear the Word of God in stillness and perhaps we may come to understand."[1]

Noise and confusion, arguments and stubbornness were the last noises Jonah had heard before he willingly jumped into the sea. The storm had been relentless. Boards began separating. Water washed over the boat.

The prophet Jonah had tried to sleep through it all. It was the type of rest that a tumultuous heart uses to grab peace for itself. It didn't work. Breaking into the hold of the ship, the captain woke Jonah in a fury. "Call on your god! Maybe your god will treat us with favor so that we will not perish" (Jonah 1:6).

It didn't seem likely. This particular God—the only God—had become angry with Jonah. The storm was his fault. So, in the midst of the furious squall, the howling wind and the foaming waves the men desperately asked the prophet: "What should we do to you, to quiet the sea that is raging against us?" (Jonah 1:11).

In order to save the other souls onboard, Jonah knew what had to be done. "Throw me into the sea" (Jonah 1:12). At once the wind died down. The waves calmed. The sea was quiet.

In order to provide that quiet, the prophet had given his life— or at least, that was probably what he thought would happen. Then came the fish. God's Word tells us that the Lord *provided* the fish for Jonah. At this point the prophet probably preferred death. Instead, God gave him silence.

This was the silence Augustine's heart yearned to find. It became the quiet he encouraged his listeners to seek out. Whether he wanted it or not, Jonah now sat in that quiet. The discipline of a storm now turned into a timeout in a fish.

No matter how much I try, I cannot picture what it would have been like for Jonah in the belly of the fish. We know he was conscious. After all, he prayed. But he was probably not able to move. Breathing must have been difficult. He probably couldn't eat—and even if he could eat he might not have wanted to.

---

[1] Donald X. Burt, "*Let Me Know You...*": Reflections on Augustine's Search for God (Collegeville, MN: Liturgical Press, 2003), 24.

He didn't admit it at first, but Jonah needed this quiet. The hub-bub of defiance and anger subsided. He could no longer avoid his God, or his sin, or his guilt. It can be a frightening experience to be alone with your thoughts—perhaps even more frightening than being swallowed alive.

Are you in a timeout right now? Has the noise died down around you? I pray you are able to find that "delightful hidden place" Augustine talked about. You need those places and those moments—frightening as they can be. You need the honesty that only silence can bring. When Augustine advises "Let us enter into ourselves" he isn't talking about finding solutions within our subconscious or some form of self-motivated salvation. He is actually saying the opposite. "Let us leave a little room for reflection in our lives." The mirror that reflection brings reveals your every sin. Stewing over that argument you had with your spouse? This silence holds it right before your face. Defiant with God over the places he expects you to go? This quiet makes sure you cannot forget it.

The pauses in our lives provide those frighteningly real moments with God's law. The expectations remain so much higher than any-thing we can achieve. The stillness forces us to face our shortcom-ings—to come to grips with our sins.

The belly of the fish in the depths of the sea furnished Jonah with the dark silence he needed in order to admit his sinfulness. He was in distress both physically and spiritually. With vivid language Jonah confesses as much, "...from the belly of the grave...into the depths...the heart of the seas...currents swept around me...I have been driven away from your sight...I was near death" (Jonah 2:2-5). The quiet does that. It places you at the bottom of your life. It forces you to see reality, every stark, horrific detail.

But silence also does so much more than that. For perhaps the first time in a long time, this arresting silence forced Jonah to realize he had nothing left. He could only look to his Lord. "In my distress I called to the Lord, and he answered me" (Jonah 2:2). We would expect Jonah to confess this later from the shore, but he said these words from the fish! "You brought my life up from the pit, O Lord, my God" (Jonah 2:6).

Then comes the moment for which all this ruckus and tumult and quiet and silence prepared the prophet—the point of the entire experience below the seas. Jonah ends his prayer by looking directly up to his loving God and confessing, "What I have vowed, I will certainly pay in full. Salvation belongs to the Lord" (Jonah 2:9).

Fitting words for a prophet who grew up only a few miles and a handful of centuries away from Jesus. The Savior himself would one day look back on this moment in Jonah's life to prophesy the greatest miracle of all. "Just as Jonah was in the belly of the huge fish for three days and three nights, so the Son of Man will be three days and three nights in the heart of the earth" (Matt 12:40). This Jesus remains the difference between the belly of a fish and dry land; the difference between darkness and light; the difference between death and life.

Your salvation comes from the Lord, too. Sometimes, the only way Jesus can make you understand the depths of your own sin is to place you in the belly of the fish. Those dark moments in your life, that silence forces you to see your sins the way God sees them. But then they point you forward to the suffering and the death and the grave and the empty tomb of your Savior.

Augustine was right. Take a moment every day to leave behind the noise and confusion. Put aside your work and your worries. They will be there when you return. And for a moment—or even two moments—hear the Word of God. That Word will provide you with stillness for the storms of your life. It will focus you on what matters most today. And it will remind you of the perfect eternity waiting for you.

Comfort for the Night

"When my life was ebbing away, I remembered the Lord" (Jonah 2:7).

CHAPTER 22

A Prophetic Sunset

Micah 3:1-8

"Darkness will come upon you, without any omens from God. The sun will set for the prophets, and daytime will become dark for them" (Mic 3:6). God often uses darkness and light metaphorically to describe the silent mouth and the spoken word. Once again the Lord speaks. He prophesies the dark end of the many false prophets parading around Israel in those days. God's people living in the eighth century B.C. had seen their share of days of light and nights of darkness. The coming shade would be their blackest night yet.

God's Church and her people have endured a long, difficult struggle with the darkness of false prophecy. In our devotions we have already journeyed through many of those horrific nights. We watched sin blacken the world in the Garden of Eden. We slept with Abraham as he experienced that frightful dream. We wrestled with the Lord alongside Jacob. Judges allowed selfishness to reign. Kings took advantage of their people. Even prophets chose their own dark recesses rather than spreading God's light.

That struggle against darkness continues in our New Testament world as well. In the three centuries after Jesus' death and resurrection, the Christian Church had gotten caught up in that battle between the light of God's Word and the dangerous lies of the devil. Persecutions spread believers across the known world. House churches sprouted up in every corner of the Roman Empire. Christians could be found serving within various levels of society: from slaves to soldiers to senators, and eventually, even emperors.

Then everything changed. Constantine the Great became the first emperor to openly declare himself a Christian. He then went on to declare Christianity an accepted religion of the Roman Empire. How far the Christian faith had come! Once persecuted Christians now saw their faith become a hallmark of the Roman Empire. It seemed the darkness Micah warned his people about eleven centuries earlier had finally acquiesced to the light of the gospel.

That's when perhaps the greatest danger in the history of Christianity reared its ugly head. It seemed with the Empire becoming Christian, many let their guard down. All sorts of false teachings rose up like weeds. Some pastors began teaching "secret truths" that they had added to God's Word. Others preached that to be a "true" Christian one had to die a martyrs' death. No sooner had "daytime" come for the Church than darkness blotted out the spiritual sun of the Roman Empire.

Every one of these false teachers and each of their false teachings threw churches into turmoil. But one man surpassed them all. His name was Arius, and his false teaching was so detrimental, and so enticing, that it sent a shockwave through the entire Christian Church—the reverberations of which can still be felt today.

History tells us that Pastor Arius appeared talk, dark and handsome. No one could preach a sermon as well as he could. He wrote music that people hummed for centuries. But while his honey-sweet appearance seemed harmless, his sermons silently stung people's souls. Arius said that because Jesus was begotten of God the Father, then he must have been *less* than God the Father.

It sounded so logical! But it was completely wrong. The problem was that thousands, and eventually millions of believers were captivated by that teaching. Arius' dark teaching seemed so bright. In fact, many who followed Arius' teaching would have asked, "What was the harm? So, Arius taught that Jesus was a little less than the Father - some passages even seemed to suggest that."

But it was a big deal. To diminish who Jesus is and what he has done, cut away at the central message of Scripture! Church councils wrestled with this Arian message for decades, until finally they arrived at a scriptural stance. I bet it sounds familiar: "We believe in one Lord, Jesus Christ, the only Son of God, eternally begotten of the Father, God from God, Light from Light, true God from true God, begotten, not made, of one being with the Father." That portion of the Nicene Creed, which we confess together in worship, had to be written and confessed because of one rogue pastor and his poisonous teaching.

Our creeds are filled with those types of stories, when complete darkness threatened the light of God's gospel message. In fact, nearly every phrase of the creeds we confess are written in blood. Each word tells a bitter story of pain, division and loss.

This remains the story of darkness and light. It is Micah's story. It is your story too.

Before the Lord called him to be his prophet, Micah must have felt surrounded by darkness. Having grown up as a small-town boy, he spent his prophetic career in the big city of Jerusalem. Talk about a culture shock! But if Jerusalem frightened Micah, we have no evidence of it.

Like the Lord himself, Micah was always more concerned with the blackness of sin and the danger false prophets posed to God's people. Here the Lord reaches as serious of a note as we ever see in Scripture. "Listen," Micah says to begin his second of three sermons. False prophets and wicked rulers rarely want to listen. The false prophets are too busy spouting off their own version of God's will. The wicked rulers opened their mouths to devour the very people they were meant to serve.

The sun was setting for Israel. The Lord was about to give the rebellious rulers and the phony prophets a dose of their own darkness. In shame and disgrace these men would finally cover their mouths.

Covering our mouths and opening our ears to listen to God's truths can be a difficult task—even for his followers. Like Micah's Jerusalem and Arius' Roman Empire, the sun appears to be setting on our world as well. The truths we hold to are coming under attack. Shade is cast your way as friends and neighbors call you out for believing that Jesus could really be God. Coworkers wonder with sin-blackened hearts why you would take off on Sunday to worship—no one seems to do that anymore.

In the face of such a terrifying night, the devil tempts us to hold back on what we believe. After all, the darkness stays away if the light of your faith doesn't shine so brightly. Warning about this sin-darkened world, Jesus once encouraged his disciples, "Do not be afraid of them, because there is nothing concealed that will not be revealed, and nothing hidden that will not be made known. What I tell you in the dark, speak in the daylight; and what you hear whispered in your ear, proclaim from the housetops" (Matt 10:26-27).

Instead we often do the opposite. We remain silent about our faith at times. We avoid persecution. We let darkness roll in, because holding the bright light of God's gospel can burn us in this world.

Micah understood how dangerous the deeds of darkness could be. Yet by God's grace he refused to hold back the light of God's word. This small-town Micah prophesied about the future events that would take place 700 years later in another small town. "You, Bethlehem Ephrathah, though you are small among the clans of Judah, from you, will go out the one who will be the ruler for me in Israel. His goings forth are from the beginning, from the days of eternity" (Mic 5:2).

The Light of the world that would shine first from those lowly Bethlehem hills would go on to shine throughout Judea. His words would kindle the fire of faith in countless others. And even when he himself would go to a cross to willingly be extinguished, he would gloriously shine again on Easter Sunday.

This Jesus, this Light of the world, remains both true man and true God. He had to be. Quite frankly, if he wasn't, then what is the point? If Jesus isn't who he says he is then we have made him out to be a liar. He couldn't be our Savior. Heaven wouldn't be ours. And all is lost.

That had been the dark reality for the millions listening to Arius 1700 years ago. He had become a type of pied piper, playing his tune of false teaching and luring the entire Christian Roman Empire away from Christ with him.

Then came along another pastor named Athanasius. Like a lone voice in a storm, he boldly preached that Jesus Christ is God. For his faithful preaching, he was exiled by the government and his church five times! He never wavered. At a gathering called the Council of Nicaea, a group of pastors put together and signed a creed that summarized who Jesus is. The secretary of that Council was Athanasius. His job was to write down the words.

And that is how it came to be that the much maligned defender of the faith wrote down the words that would eventually form our Nicene Creed. We still confess these words to this very day. The light of God's gospel chased away the shadows of false teaching.

These are not empty words we confess. They are God's word. And not even the darkness can envelop them.

Comfort for the Night

"So do not be afraid of them, because there is nothing concealed that will not be revealed, and nothing hidden that will not be made known. What I tell you in the dark, speak in the daylight; and what you hear whispered in your ear, proclaim from the housetops" (Matt 10:26-27).

CHAPTER 23

The Dead of Night

2 Chronicles 32

"Fear of man will prove to be a snare, but whoever trusts in the Lord is kept safe" (Prov 29:25). King Hezekiah had a most difficult choice placed in front of him. He probably would not have wished it on anyone. Either he would give into his fear and let the invading Assyrians take over Jerusalem, or he would trust in the Lord and fight one of the most ruthless armies history has ever seen.

In his heart of hearts Hezekiah might have thought to himself, "You know, I don't deserve this." Hezekiah was a good king. He was a faithful king. He had destroyed the high places and removed the false gods from his kingdom. He repaired the temple and restored the order of worship of the true God. He had done everything he was supposed to do as a king. But the enemy came anyway.

"After all that Hezekiah had so faithfully done, Sennacherib king of Assyria came and invaded Judah. He laid siege to the fortified cities, thinking to conquer them for himself" (2 Chr 32:1).[1] Having removed the enemies from within, it was time for Hezekiah to face the enemies from outside Jerusalem's walls. And Sennacherib certainly stood as a formidable foe.

The entire northern kingdom of Israel had just fallen to Sennacherib. In fact, it seemed like every nation had acquiesced to the Assyrian commander. But the Assyrians weren't just master warriors. They were ruthless conquerers. When they defeated a nation

---

[1] The Holy Bible, New International Version (Saint Louis: Concordia Publishing House, 1984), 661.

they would behead many of the people and pile their heads into a pyramid at their city gate. Assyria did not just destroy their enemies. They made them scream in agony.

And Jerusalem was next.

It wasn't enough for a nation to simply know the Assyrians were coming. Sennacherib sends a written warning to King Hezekiah and the people of Jerusalem. "What are you relying on as you sit there under siege in Jerusalem?" (2 Chr 32:10). Then comes the Assyrian history lesson. "Don't you know what I and my fathers have done to all the people of the other lands? Were the gods of those foreign nations ever able to deliver their land from my hand?" (2 Chr 32:13).

It was enough to make even the bravest warrior's knees weak. And so, King Hezekiah had a choice to make. Would he give into fear and open Jerusalem's doors? Would he trust in the Lord and stand against this ruthless army?

Hezekiah's choice was a decisive one. He had the people of Jerusalem assemble. Then he commanded his military officers to speak these words, "Be strong. Be courageous. Do not be afraid. Do not be terrified because of the presence of the king of Assyria and the horde that is with him, because the one with us is greater than all those who are with him" (2 Chr 32:7).

Sennacherib arrived with his entire army and the siege began.

There are times when God seems hidden—when he appears nowhere to be seen. Those are precisely the moments when he is giving you your greatest opportunity to trust in him. For King Hezekiah and the rest of God's people in Jerusalem, the Lord certainly seemed hidden as they watched the Assyrians surround their city.

On Palm Sunday we watch another man marching on Jerusalem. He wasn't a ruthless dictator, nor was he accompanied by an army of hundreds of thousands of men. He didn't ride on a war-horse or a chariot for battle. He was and remains the Son of God, yet he approached Jerusalem atop nothing but a peaceful donkey. His entourage was twelve disciples. And having seen their fair share of conquering rulers march through Jerusalem, God's people couldn't be happier in seeing Jesus, their peaceful king, come.

"Look, your King comes to you, humble, and riding on a donkey, on a colt, the foal of a donkey" (Matt 21:5). The Gospel of Matthew tells us how this march of Jesus into Jerusalem looked. "A very large crowd spread their outer clothing on the road. Others were cutting branches from the trees and spreading them out on the road" (Matt 21:8). And the crowds weren't silent. "[They] kept shouting, 'Hosanna to the Son of David! Blessed is he who comes in the name of the Lord!'" (Matt 21:9).

It was a march to murder and the people didn't even realize it. Jesus wasn't coming into Jerusalem to conquer her. He wasn't even coming to Jerusalem to lead her. He was coming to die. As the hymn states, "Ride on, ride on in majesty! In lowly pomp ride on to die."[2]

Jesus' destination wasn't the kingly throne. It was the cruel cross.

As far as torture devices go, the cross might just be the worst of them all. Do you know who invented it? It wasn't the Romans, although they seem to have perfected the gruesome apparatus. No, it was the Assyrians. Those brutal, ruthless armies not only wanted to conquer the world, they wanted everyone to shriek in torment.

Those very Assyrians now surrounded King Hezekiah. The city now sat as a solitary island, separated from the rest of the world by an ocean of Assyrians. In addition to their battle prowess and brutality, the Assyrians were master manipulators. To further frighten Jerusalem's king, it seems quite possible that Sennacherib would have had a cross constructed within the sight of Hezekiah's walls, complete with his name at the top.

The Lord had told his king, "Do not be afraid of these words which you heard" (2 Kgs 19:6). He had promised Jerusalem's leader, "I will protect and save this city" (2 Kgs 19:34). But when the enemy surrounds your city, fear quickly descends on even the strongest of hearts behind the walls.

What would be going through your mind if you stood on those walls, watching Assyrian soldiers crying out for blood? What do you think was going through Jesus' mind as he heard the shouts of Hosanna, knowing they would turn into shouts of "crucify him" just days later?

How afraid do you get when God seems "hidden"?

It is tempting to give up in moments like that. Maybe you have considered throwing in the towel when the world surrounds you and

---

[2] Wisconsin Evangelical Lutheran Synod, *Christian Worship*, "Ride on, Ride On in Majesty" (Milwaukee: Northwestern Publishing House, 1993), 133.

cuts you off. When your enemies are waiting for your demise, it can be easy to give in. That choice standing before Hezekiah—to fear Assyria or fear the Lord—may not be a choice we envy. Yet that choice finds you more often than you would like.

"Do I trust in my own strength to get myself out of this problem or do I trust in the Lord?" The question rattles around in our head when obstacles pile up. But here is the thing: In those most difficult moments, God gives you great opportunity to live by faith. That remains especially true when God seems hidden.

Listen to Hezekiah's faithful encouragement for his people. "With [the king of Assyria] is only an arm of flesh. With us is the Lord our God to help us and to fight our battles" (2 Chr 32:8). And that's just what God did.

"Hezekiah the king and Isaiah son of Amoz, the prophet, prayed about this, crying out to heaven. So the Lord sent an angel, who wiped out all the powerful warriors, the commanders, and the officers in the camp of the king of Assyria" (2 Chr 32:20-21). The Assyrians lost almost 200,000 men that night. Hezekiah and his people remained alive. Salvation for Jerusalem had come from the Lord.

Salvation for the world was coming through Christ. That colt faithfully trudged on over the people's cloaks and the palm branches. It dutifully carried the Savior to his destruction - a destruction that had to take place for your salvation.

King Hezekiah might just have witnessed an Assyrian cross with his name on it. Jesus certainly saw his name on that Roman instrument of death. His name was written over yours. Jesus removed your name from that cross in order to write it in blood upon his book of life.

And yet, strife remains in our day to day lives. Enemies will still surround you. Their propaganda-like words will cut to your soul with a dagger of doubt. *Can I escape this? Why does God seem so hidden tonight?*

Take heart, fellow child of God! Listen to the speech an old king from a bygone era speaks God's comfort to you. "Be strong. Be courageous. Do not be afraid. Do not be terrified" (2 Chr 32:7). And then remember why you can have peace...even tonight...

Comfort for the Night

"The one with us is greater than all those who are with him" (2 Chr 32:7).

CHAPTER 24

The Pitch Black Pit

Daniel 6:18

I wonder if Darius the Mede ever got a good night's sleep. Had you been seated on his Persian throne managing an empire of kingdoms, your head would probably never hit the pillow either. No wonder then that it seemed like a good idea for Darius to appoint so many satraps underneath his three grand supervisors. Many hands make light work.

But that wasn't what kept the Persian king awake on this night. His empire would still be around in the morning. However, his trusted supervisor, Daniel, wouldn't be. At that very moment the old Jewish administrator, who so many years ago had been forcefully relocated from his Jerusalem home, sat in a sealed den of lions. No one had ever survived such a punishment. No one *could* survive. That was the point.

The king's mind must have poured over every detail that led to that night. His own supervisors and satraps had approached him with an innocent-sounding request. After the fact, Darius probably kicked himself for not smelling a rat. After all, how often do so many administrators throughout an empire agree on religious policies? The written document had come too quickly. Had he only taken more time to think through the ramifications of the unchangeable law he signed into existence!

After the king passed the law, the administrators immediately informed on one of their own. "Daniel, who is one of the exiles from Judah, does not pay attention to you" (Dan 6:13). Administrative jealousy lurked beneath their proclamation. The king should have seen it earlier. "Three times each day [Daniel] is praying his prayers" (Dan 6:13).

Daniel knew the law as well as anyone. Tirelessly working for various administrations most of his life, he had outlasted both kings and kingdoms. Immediately after he heard that this prayer-law had passed, he rushed home…to *pray*. His rivals couldn't believe it—Daniel had fallen right into their trap. What a politically foolish move!

What an example of faith.

Thinking over the events of the day during his dark night, Darius must have poured over Daniel's final moments. It is not too often in life when you know you are seeing a friend for the last time. Daniel's calm walk into that cave of death must have surprised the king. Viewing the old Jewish man from above, the king perhaps watched his face until that very last moment when the stone fully covered the mouth.

No amount of entertainment or delicious food could pull Darius' mind away from the death sentence he had carried out that day. Even sleep eluded him. To be responsible for the gruesome death of a faithful and upright man must have torn apart Darius' heart. Guilt kept the fires going in his bedroom all night.

What horrendous guilt keeps your lights on in the middle of the night? Who did you throw to the lions? Maybe, like Darius, it was an accident. You crashed your car into someone, sending their life, and countless others connected to that life, spiraling into pain and sadness. Perhaps your betrayal was personal. You coldly tore apart a former friend's reputation—reasoning at the time that she had it coming.

We can be rather adept at keeping ourselves too busy for guilt during the day. But how do you shut your mind off when the sun goes down? You can't eat your way through your guilt. No amount of entertainment can make you forget how you wronged that person.

If only you could sleep.

Insomnia might just be one of the worst ailments a person can experience. It doesn't kill you all at once. It takes you slowly, painfully, methodically. Minute by minute, hour by hour the sweetness of sleep shortens until finally it steals away its restful trance from you completely. That's when your mind burns out. Your awake reality starts to merge with your dream world. The human brain struggles to distinguish the two. Eventually, the lack of rest slips a person into the ultimate sleep of death.

Darius was not concerned about his own life—not that night. All he could think about was the poor old man in the cave. If those lions were going to rip Daniel apart, they would have done it hours ago. But maybe…just maybe, the God to whom Daniel so faithfully prayed could help.

While the king nervously paced in the darkness, Daniel could sleep soundly. He knew by faith what his comrades had confessed years earlier, "Since our God, whom we serve, does exist, he is able to save us" (Dan 3:17). Daniel also understood the other side of that confession: "But if [God] does not…"

Like Jesus sleeping on the boat in the middle of a Galilean storm, Daniel closed his eyes with a faith that looks to his Lord for protection, for comfort and for salvation. Either God would save him immediately from those lions or he would save him eternally from the world. The very prayers that put him in that lions' den now echoed off the cave walls and rang through the ears of those wild animals.

I have to admit, during my long nights of guilt and sorrow, sleep isn't the only thing that eludes me. Prayer keeps its distance too. Two dangerous extremes constantly threaten to push my prayers away— even during those blackest of moments. Guilt is the first. "Why would God ever listen to me after I hurt someone else? I don't deserve to be able to talk to God, not when I have betrayed those close to me."

Anger is the second extreme. "Why would I even want to talk to God after the evils of today? He doesn't deserve my pleading." Anger this strong takes aim at God only as a distraction. When anger wells up in our hearts, it fires at everyone else in an effort to take the blame off of ourselves. I often direct my anger at others because I feel guilt rising up from deep within my own heart.

So, there you sit, watching the moon slowly creep across the sky waiting for a sunrise that feels as though it will never arrive. The poor souls who have become the objects of our rage and betrayal seem so distant, yet they hold such a grip on our hearts. All we can do is sigh. And cry.

Eventually the morning sun peeked over the hill. Stars disappeared. The moon faded. Darkness could not help but slink away. Light flooded over the earth. A woman arrived, hoping against hope that the man doomed to death beneath a rock might possibly be alive. The stone that kept him in was rolled away. Any sign of death rolled away with it. Where was the man the rulers and administrators had turned against? Where was the one sentenced to death?

He was alive.

Turning around through tears she heard his voice. She didn't expect to ever hear it again. She knew it was him. He spoke to her by name, like he had done so many times before: "Mary" (John 20:16). Then she finally saw him—the one who was dead but now stood before her alive again. Mary saw Jesus.

King Darius must have felt like Mary Magdalene on Easter Sunday. He too rushed to a place of death, hoping against all hope that the one sentenced to a gruesome death would somehow still be alive. He had the stone rolled away. Nervously the king called down into that lion-filled cave. And for the first time in the history…an answer came back out from a den of lions.

"Your Majesty, may you live forever! My God sent his angel and shut the mouth of the lions" (Dan 6:21-22). Not a scratch on the old, well-rested Daniel. Quieted lions sat around him. The king's long night of worry finally ended. At that very moment the book of Daniel gives us a glimpse into Darius' heart: "The king was very glad" (Dan 6:23).

Your guilt might still be causing you insomnia. Sleep doesn't always come easy—even to the most faithful of believers. But your Savior does. Place all of your guilt, all of your worries at the foot of his cross. Let your mouth slip you into the sweet sleep of a child talking in bed to his Father.

Tomorrow you can rise with the sun, walking out of the tomb with your risen Savior.

Comfort for the Night

"He is the living God, who endures forever. His kingdom will not be destroyed, and his dominion is eternal. He rescues and he saves" (Dan 6:26-27).

CHAPTER 25

Peering Into The Twilight

Zechariah 1:7-6:8

Rays of sunlight glinted off the silver circlet. Gold vibrantly reflected around those gathered. The prophet's shaking hands carried the newly forged crown toward the head of Jerusalem's next king. Fittingly, this next monarch of God's people was man named "Joshua," a name designating him as a type of savior for his people. Even more felicitous was Joshua's other office. He was the high priest of God's people.

It had been a long time since a man wore a kingly crown in Jerusalem. The last man to don the crown witnessed the destruction of Jerusalem, the obliteration of the temple and the murder of his sons. It was the last thing King Zedekiah saw. Soon after, the Babylonians poked out his eyes. The royal diadem fell that day, leaving God's people kingless...and directionless.

All that was in the past now. The new temple of God's people slowly rose up on the heights of their city. God was speaking to them through their prophets again, men like Haggai and Zechariah. And most glorious of all, their high priest, their "savior" was about to be crowned king. This crown would not be the turban of a priest. This diadem placed atop Joshua's head would gleam with gold and silver.

Perhaps not since Zadok the priest had crowned Solomon had God's people witnessed such a glorious connection between king and priest. And if anyone originally present missed the important connection, God himself points it out through the prophet Zechariah: "He will be clothed with majesty, and he will sit and rule on his throne. He will be a priest on his throne" (Zech 6:13).

Zechariah must have thought this day would never come. The night before, the Lord came upon his prophet in a series of night visions more terrifying and confusing than any prophet had experienced up to that moment in history. Across one long evening, Zechariah watched the wide-awake nightmare, as the Lord choreographed vision after vision of times and days yet to arrive.

It all started in darkness. A man rode a red horse among the bows of the myrtle trees. As Zechariah peered at the man, an angel began to lead the frightened prophet through the trees. The proclamation from the Lord encompassed both anger and comfort—anger at the other nations, and comfort for his people in Jerusalem.

Immediately, the horses and myrtle trees gave way to four imposing horns. Four empires possessed the strength of horns like these, and all of them had taken their turns conquering God's people. A frightened Zechariah faced them all. Four craftsmen followed and, against all odds, terrified the conquering countries and threw them down.

Like the fluid scenes of a dream, a man walked past the pieces of horns with a measuring line. He was measuring where the walls would no longer need to be. The city whose walls still lay crumbled, would no longer need them. In the place of stone would burn a wall of fire sent from God himself. In the midst of the frightful sight, God tells his people a surprising message—one they had not heard for many years, "Shout and be glad, O Daughter of Zion. For I am coming, and I will live among you" (Zech 2:10).

Then arrived the man everyone had been waiting for: Joshua. Zechariah watched as God's high priest stood in a type of courtroom. Accusations echoed off the walls, originating from none other than Satan himself. Every sin, every despicable deed the priest had ever done was thrown in his face. Then came the new, clean garments to replace those made filthy by his sins.

Again that night, the angel woke Zechariah up. This time a vision of a golden lamp stand appeared before him. Seven candles glowed in the darkness, indicating that the power of God, not the power of his people, would protect Israel.

Suddenly, above the lamp stand a flying scroll pierced the frightful night. It was immense—the size of the temple! It warned of curses against those who broke God's law by stealing and swearing falsely.

After the scroll a basket full of wickedness went forth, topped by a cover made of lead. Two winged women came forward and flew the basket to Babylon. Judgment was coming for those who exiled Israel.

In the distance, bronze mountains arose. Out from behind them roared four powerful chariots. Colored horses impatiently pulled them to the four corners of the earth. The angel narrated the frightening scene for Zechariah, showing him that these horsemen carried out the command of the Lord: "Go! Range throughout the earth" (Zech 6:7).

All at once the visions ended. No goodbye. No concluding message. The chariots rolled away. Then came the silence.

What was the prophet supposed to make of all of these startling sights? Colored horsemen riding among myrtle trees and men measuring; golden lamp stands and flying scrolls; baskets of wickedness and imposing charioteers—and even Satan himself!

Had it all been a dream, Zechariah could have at least looked forward to being awoken. But these were not dreams. They were the draining, nightmarish prophecies of what the Lord was doing and would do in the future.

It is often during the night when our minds pull us into thoughts of the future. While no evening thought may seem as strange or haunting as Zechariah's visions from the Lord, your worries and anxieties can be just as daunting. Isn't it during those long, dark hours when you wonder about the future your children will have in a world like this? Doesn't lying on your back force you to contemplate the inevitability of your own mortality? Can you hear the guilt of your heart whispering reminders of the punishment you should have coming toward you?

You don't need visions from the Lord to keep you wide awake at night. Your own regrets can do that on their own. And often your own nighttime contemplations become the nightmare themselves.

But did you catch the gospel God built into each of Zechariah's visions? Each horrifying scene shocked the law into Zechariah's heart…and ours. But each oracle ended with good news. The man on his red horse haunted the myrtle trees, but then proclaimed consolation for Jerusalem. The four powerful horns that scattered God's people would themselves be cast down. The man ominously measuring the absence of a wall to protect God's people pointed to a wall of fire that the Lord would use to protect his people. Satan comes to accuse Joshua the high priest of the filthiness of his sins, only to be defeated by the robes of righteousness that God perfectly fits on him. A glowing lamp stand lights the way for God's people, bookended by two anointed men called to carry out God's work among his people. A flying scroll warns of the punishment sin incurs, and a basket of wickedness is carried away to Babylon. Four chariots suddenly, and frighteningly roar through the earth, but only as a sign that God rules all things for the good of those who love him.

I'm not sure God expects you to remember each vivid detail of Zechariah's nighttime visions. Satan's accusations and the flying scroll of the law and the basket of wickedness are real enemies that slip into our nighttime bedrooms. So often they have convinced us that we have no hope.

God's people felt the same way. Their darkness and guilt and punishment felt eternal. The long night never seemed to end for Israel.

But Zechariah's long night did end. The sun rose again. And the light glinted off of a new crown, meant for a new king. There Joshua stood, a high priest and a king all rolled into one. Zechariah stood there too, a prophet of God's returned people. Together those two pointed ahead to the coming prophet who would perfectly preach to his people. They looked ahead to the coming High Priest, who would sacrifice himself for the world, once for all. And the crown that was placed on Joshua's head rested as a shadow of the crown that Jesus now wears as he rules in your heart.

Soon this dark night will be over. Tomorrow the sun with shine again. Your King has come. He hasn't forgotten you the way worldly kings might. In fact, he makes sure that what is best for you shall come to pass. And one day you will see him in all of his glory—the glory Zechariah described for you. "He will be clothed with majesty, and he will sit and rule on his throne. He will be a priest on his throne." And he will clothe you with perfection, bringing you into his eternal kingdom of daylight.

Comfort for the Night

"Just as you once were a curse among the nations, O house of Judah and house of Israel, so now I will save you. You will be a blessing. Do not be afraid. Let your hands be strong" (Zech 8:13).

CHAPTER 26

Ezra's Fast in the Shadows

Ezra 10:1-6

Ask any pastor what he dreads the most and you will probably get variations of the same basic answer: "I don't dread anything. Ministry is a pleasure!" Then ask him again, and after a sigh he'll give you the real response: "I dread confronting members living in sin."

The couple who has just started coming back to church catches your pastor after the Sunday service to ask him a quick request: "We're engaged! We would be honored if you could do the service next summer." It certainly is an honor for a pastor to receive that request. Really, it is.

But your pastor also knows there is a good chance a secret is lurking under the surface of their innocent-looking smiles. He hopes with all of his heart it isn't true, but these days the chances are very good that it probably is. Once the couple's pre-marriage counseling classes begin the truth finally comes out.

They're living together.

I just sighed out loud typing the words. Maybe your heart sighed reading them. Or perhaps you simply don't know what the big deal is. After all, aren't they in love? And aren't they going to get married by a pastor in a church?

Those are all good things. But this couple remains in danger—at that very moment. They are putting their eternal lives on the line. The sin they are living in is a consistent, every-day refusal to repent.

You need to know that this is not my opinion. God states this. It is how he established his loving gift of marriage. "Marriage is to be held in honor by all, and the marriage bed is to be kept undefiled, for

God will judge sexually immoral people and adulterers" (Heb 13:7). God loves you too much to see you walking toward hell in the name of love.

But that is a tough conversation to have with a young couple in love. Even under the best of circumstances the future husband and wife can storm out of the pastor's office, never to be seen again. It doesn't always end that way, but many times it does. It makes your pastor's heart weep every time.

Ezra spent one long night weeping for the couples he was pastoring. His sadness led to fasting and mourning through the evening. On behalf of his people he had thrown himself down in front of God's house. I don't think any pastor would envy Ezra's situation. His congregation was coming apart, and it all had to do with marriage.

God's people had returned from exile, happy to begin anew again in their promised land. They built houses and re-established their cities. And they got married. At first the countryside might have resembled America after World War II. Families and communities merged together under a unified banner.

But a crack was forming in the foundation of many of these marriages. The book of Ezra explains, "The people of Israel and the priests and the Levites have not separated themselves from the peoples of the lands" (Ezra 9:1). Many other peoples had repopulated the lands around Jerusalem. Instead of finding wives among their own people, God's people had intermarried with the unbelievers around them.

Having surveyed the disastrous situation, Ezra does what any loving pastor would do on behalf of his people. He prayed. "My God, I am ashamed and too embarrassed to lift my face to you, my God, because our sinful deeds have risen above our heads" (Ezra 9:6). Ezra placed himself with his people—the shepherd standing among his sheep looking to the Lord.

This might all sound extreme to us sitting in the New Testament. But God had been crystal clear with his Old Testament people regarding marriage. At the end of their Exodus, as they stood on the precipice of Canaan, the Lord commanded his Israelites to watch out for the idolatrous Canaanite peoples living there. "Do not form marriage alliances with them. Do not give your daughters to their sons, and do not take their daughters for your sons" (Deut 7:3). Then, in love, the Lord explained why this command remained so vitally important.

"Because they will turn your sons away from following me, and they will serve other gods" (Deut 7:4).

It had happened before. In the days of Noah, God used the lens of marriage to describe how wicked the world had become, "The sons of God saw that the daughters of men were beautiful, and they took as wives for themselves any of them they chose" (Gen 6:2). Ezra saw his people making the same mistakes that years earlier had led to the great deluge!

Hundreds of Israelites were living in sin even though they were married. What was Ezra to do? Pastors today are tempted to look the other way when a couple is living in sin. Family members do the same. And we can become rather adept at explaining these sins away. "Well, at least they love each other, and they're getting married anyway." And the law becomes silent in order to keep a relationship happy.

But this isn't love. Love makes time for the difficult conversation. Love politely, patiently shares God's will in marriage. And love holds out hope that the couple storming out today might yet return some day.

Ezra must have sighed as he tossed and turned during the long night. His congregation, his people had been living in sin. It was time for love to share God's law. Once everyone was gathered before him, the pastor lovingly had the difficult conversation with his people: "You have been unfaithful and have married foreign wives...So now, give praise to the Lord, the God of your fathers, and do his will—separate yourselves from the peoples of the land and from your foreign wives" (Ezra 10:10-11).

Separating families? Is this really what a loving God would want? It seems some of the men standing before Ezra refused—perhaps with these very objections. Had we been standing in that massive group of men we might have questioned Ezra as well.

But Ezra stood with the Lord. How sad that these Jewish people had intermarried. Their sins had caused generational pain. It can be the same for people living in sin today. The consequences may not be felt right away, but over time the small-looking snowball of sin eventually causes an avalanche of other problems.

At the pleading of their loving leader, the Jews realized that their marriages had been invalid from the beginning. They had disobeyed God. Now it was time for Israel to repent and live in that repentance.

Jesus never said that living according to his word would be easy. In fact, he warned that it would divide families. Whether you are a pastor or not, these conversations remain difficult. But show the love that Jesus did by starting those talks. Think of all the difficult conversations he began with the sinners around him: "Go, call your husband…" (John 4:16) or "I came to turn a man against his father…" (Matt 10:34) or even "from now on do not sin anymore…" (John 8:11).

Your Savior's difficult discussions led to some of those unbelievers putting their faith in him. They also led to vengeance and anger, and his own suffering and death. But your Savior understood that each of these conversations is a word of love toward someone living on the edge of hell. And that's who Jesus came for, a world on the edge of hell. He paid for all of their sins…and yours.

In a world where persecution can come from within your own family, where love is often absent from the tough conversations, take hold of Jesus' words. Share his truth, and share it with love.

Comfort for the Night

"Do not worry about how you will defend yourself, or what you will say, for the Holy Spirit will teach you in that very hour what you should say" (Luke 12:11-12).

CHAPTER 27

Nehemiah's Midnight Ride

Nehemiah 2:1-16

On the evening of August 18, 1805, a young man sat down in the foothills of Colorado to write in his journal. The occasion should have been a happy one—the man was celebrating his 31st birthday. But on this evening melancholy supplanted joy. In solemnity he penned some of the saddest words he would ever write: "This day I completed my thirty first year, and conceived that I had in all human probability now existed about half the period which I am to remain in this Sublunary world. I reflected that I had as yet done but little, very little indeed, to further the happiness of the human race, or to advance the information of the succeeding generation."[1]

The man who wrote those words was none other than Meriwether Lewis. The night he wrote them might have been the longest of his life. President Thomas Jefferson had sent him and his Corp of Discovery to find a water passage from the Mississippi to the Pacific. Along with his companion, William Clark, Lewis had faced friendly tribes of Native Americans and dangerous enemies. They had nearly lost their lives on multiple occasions. And now, a seemingly impassable collection of rocky mountains towered over them. Thousands of miles away from home, they stood at the edge of the map, ready to head into the unknown.

In Lewis' estimation they had failed. There was no northwest passage. Countless mountains towered before them. The Native

---

[1] Ed. Reuben Gold Thwaites, *Original journals of the Lewis and Clark Expedition, 1804-1806 Vol. 2* (New York: Dodd, Mead & Company, 1904), 368.

American tribe that was supposed to give them a collection of much needed horses was nowhere to be found. If they didn't find that tribe before the winter snows fell they would all die in the mountains. Lewis and his men were staring directly at death. And if they failed, it would all be his fault.

On the night of his 31st birthday, Lewis assessed the entire situation—as any man does on his birthday in the middle of his life. At the nadir of his journey he looked both forward and backward. This is where his mind took him that night as he wrote in his journal...

"I viewed with regret the many hours I have spent in indolence, and now sorely feel the want of that information which those hours would have given me had they been judiciously expended."

Did a Lewis-like melancholy darken Nehemiah's soul as he waited on the king? It must have. Normally, Nehemiah would not reveal such strong emotions in the king's presence. Yet somber emotions often find their way out of even the most securely locked hearts.

"This must be sadness in your heart," King Artaxerxes deciphered (Neh 2:2). He was right. Now Nehemiah was afraid. Men had died for showing far less emotion in the presence of kings. Yet on this day Nehemiah showed bravery. Perhaps his sadness pushed him into uncharacteristic boldness. "Why shouldn't I look sad when the city, the place of my ancestors' tombs, lies in ruins, and its gates have been consumed by fire?" (Neh 2:3).

Then Nehemiah said a silent prayer to the Lord. He would be as ruined as his country without the help of his God. And the Lord heard Nehemiah's prayer. The king acquiesced. He gave the servant of the Lord everything he needed, and Nehemiah was quick to explain why: "The king gave them to me, because the good hand of my God was upon me" (Neh 2:8).

After a long journey, Nehemiah finally arrived at home. The sight was worse than he could have ever imagined. To take it all in, he made a midnight assessment of the damage his city of Jerusalem had sustained during the years of captivity.

Like Meriwether Lewis lamenting in his journal, Nehemiah records the somber sights he witnessed during his night ride. "I began inspecting the walls of Jerusalem, which had been breached, and its gates, which had been consumed by fire" (Neh 2:13). Perhaps

Nehemiah needed that time alone in the dark to come to grips with Jerusalem's sad reality. There are times when the night can reveal more than the daylight.

Do you need darkness to assess the destruction in your life? Sometimes the light needs to go away to allow for the stillness of night to sober our thoughts. But beware—the devil and his demons do not take the night off. They work to tempt you with guilt and loneliness in the middle of the night, too.

As you take in the smoldering ruins of the consequences of your sins, your sinful nature brings up feelings of guilt. The words you have said can't be taken back. The people you have pushed away may never return. As you ride along through the broken memories of your sinful past a Nehemiah-like lament might soon cover you. These memories cannot be changed. You cannot fix your past any more than Nehemiah could go back and prevent the Babylonians from bashing in Jerusalem's walls.

But Jesus did.

Centuries after Nehemiah's midnight ride, Jesus himself rode into Jerusalem on a colt. Nothing about his humble ride was hidden. The crowds cheered. The rulers fell silent. Celebration ensued.

But Jesus knew what was coming.

Outside those piles of rubble that Nehemiah rode through, Jesus himself suffered the longest night of anyone. Rejected, betrayed and alone, Jesus suffered the death of a criminal. He endured the hell of sinners...for all sinners. The guilt you feel in those lonely midnight moments over the words you have flung at others or the actions you cannot take back have been paid for. Forever. Jesus died for them all.

Have you reached your 31st birthday yet? Perhaps it was many years ago. That milestone was an important and sobering night for Meriwether Lewis. He had felt a failure. His life and the lives of those entrusted to him hung in the balance.

Then, as if back from the dead, Lewis completely changed the tone of his journal entry. "I dash from me the gloomy thought and resolved in future, to redouble my exertions and at least endeavour to promote those two primary objects of human existence, by giving them the aid of that portion of talents which nature and fortune have bestowed on me; or in future, to live for mankind, as I have heretofore lived for myself."[2]

Lewis returned to his American optimism just in time. Within days they found the Native Americans they were looking for. They traded for the horses they so desperately needed. They successfully crossed the treacherous terrain. And eventually, they even reached the Pacific Ocean and returned home safely. The journey was anything but a failure. It stands as one of the greatest American success stories in our nation's history.

Nehemiah had an even greater task before him. The man who prayed before a king now became Jerusalem's encourager: "Let's get up and rebuild!" (Neh 2:18).

Let those words be your encouragement, too.

Your nighttime journeys through the smoldering ruins of your past need not shatter you. Those sins are forgiven. Really, they are. All of them. And in the glow of such an all-encompassing forgiveness, the Lord sends you out to the walls of his kingdom with a Nehemiah-like encouragement, "Let's get up and rebuild!"

The people you love are struggling with guilt during the night, too. Share that good news of sins forgiven with them. Pray for them. Encourage your friends with the encouragement you yourself received from God's nighttime rider…

Comfort for the Night

"The God of Heaven will make us successful. We, his servants, will rise up…" (Neh 2:20).

---

[2] Thwaites, 368.

CHAPTER 28

Centuries of Silence

Daniel 11:21-24

Fear and anger must have caused Judas more long nights than he could remember. But one particular night probably stuck in his mind. As the leader of a small, ragtag band of Jews, all he had to do was look on the faces of his meager force. They were hanging on by a thread. The next morning would reveal the sad truth: They were about to march against a professional force that was twice their size. An experienced Greek general would be marching against their inexperienced group. Judas didn't stand a chance.

But Judas Maccabeus had the night to think it over. As he and his men prepared for their epic battle, thoughts of Greek atrocities must have run through their minds. Problems were nothing new for the Jews of Judas' day. In fact, trouble seemed to have followed their ancestors all the way home from their Babylonian captivity. Conqueror after conqueror had imposed his will on God's people. Armies had turned Judas' beloved Judean landscape from a destination into a highway for conquerors.

Even Judas' hometown of Jerusalem, the city they were defending, paled in comparison to the glory and brilliance that once emanated from her. The temple looked like a shell of what it once was. The Jewish people seemed to number fewer and appear weaker every year.

But Judas didn't put together his army for any of those reasons. Darker times had descended upon his people. A smooth-talking, despicable king named Antiochus IV had come to power over Judas' people. And this wicked king was going to do whatever he could to turn God's Jewish people into Gentile Greeks.

The book of 1 Maccabees, a historical account of what happened to God's people between Malachi and Matthew, vividly details the atrocities Israel faced. "The king wrote to his whole kingdom that all should be one people and that each should give up his customs" (Macc 1:41-42).[1] That's when Antiochus really got to work. He forbade all temple sacrifices and the celebration of the important Jewish feasts. He commanded the building of Greek altars in the place where God's altar stood. He told the Jews to sacrifice swine and other unclean animals instead of lambs and bulls. He even outlawed circumcision.

Now to be sure, many kings had turned God's people away from their religious practices over the years. Where Antiochus' suppression surpassed them was in his intense knowledge of Jewish customs. Other kings might simply push aside the entire Jewish covenant. Yet Antiochus made a point to flip each Old Testament ordinance on its head. Festivals like the Passover were silenced. Greek altars displaced Jewish ones. Pigs were sacrificed in place of lambs.

Then came the violence. "Where the book of the covenant was found in the possession of anyone or if anyone adhered to the law, the decree of the king condemned him to death" (Macc 1:57). Antiochus didn't just have men punished. "They put to death the women who had their children circumcised and their families and those who circumcised them" (Macc 1:60-61). The scared, weeping faces of their dying loved ones must have hovered before each of Judas' men that night. "They hung the infants from their mothers' necks" (Macc 1:61). How could they ever forget the heart-wrenching deeds the king and his men carried out among their children?

Some Jews escaped Antiochus' tyranny. Many died trying to flee Jerusalem. Resolutely, the Jewish people banded together in the hills of the wilderness. That's when Judas Maccabeus took charge. He had won a series of skirmishes against their Greek oppressors. Many who sat with Judas on the night before their epic battle had been with him from the beginning.

King Antiochus and the Greeks began to fear this Jew and his undefeated men. So, they brought in their big guns: 40,000 infantry and 7,000 cavalry. Their orders were to leave the Jewish region a

---

[1] General Editor Edward Engelbrecht, *The Apocrypha* (St. Louis: Concordia Publishing House, 2012), 162.

smoldering husk. Now only Judas and his little group stood in their way.

What does an outnumbered and overmatched commander say to his men on the eve of an impending loss? What does the commander say to himself? Their very lives had been placed in his hands. The lives of his entire Jewish people rested behind his shield.

It must have been the longest night Judas ever endured.

Have you sat on the eve of battle, waiting to face off against a powerful enemy? A soldier can readily recall those moments of calm before the storm. But even if you have never stepped foot on a physical battle field, you've experienced those long nights before facing off against a much more powerful person.

Tomorrow you finally see that sibling you've been avoiding for years. What memories flash through you mind during your sleepless night? You have been waiting to talk to the doctor about a possible serious illness, but don't feel bold enough to go through with it. What do you tell yourself during that long evening before going? Perhaps your long night is made longer by temptation. How can you talk yourself out of falling into your pet sins?

The book of 1 Maccabees doesn't tell us what Judas was thinking that night before the battle, but it does tell us what he said to his men. "Gird yourselves and be valiant. Be ready early in the morning to fight with these Gentiles who have assembled against us to destroy us and our sanctuary" (1 Macc 3:58).

Did Jesus think back to Judas' long night as he passed through Mizpah in his ministry? After all, Jesus knew the long odds they faced. He understood better than anyone the angst they felt as they prepared to oppose their enemies. Jesus felt that same angst the night before he opposed his enemies. He traveled to a place of prayer with his small group of men. The odds looked long for him, too.

But none of that was what made that Thursday night Jesus' longest on earth. The cross loomed on the horizon. Sin and the devil and hell and death waited for him on the battlefield outside Jerusalem's walls. He would walk out against them all. He would do it alone.

Nights before grand battles seem to invite introspection. Those moments pull you in, don't they? You look back on the life you have lived. You sigh at the many sins you still remember. You groan at the trouble tomorrow will bring. And then you wait in-between the two—the calm that the eye of the storm brings.

Resolutely, Jesus walked straight into his battle against sin, death and the devil. He faced jeers with silence. He met murder with peace. He gave up his life into death...to win eternal life for you.

Judas Maccabeus looked forward to just such a Messiah. As he waited for his promised Savior, he knew he needed to fight for the physical and spiritual lives of his people. That's why, in the face of such overwhelming odds, Judas encouraged his men with these words: "It is better for us to die in battle than to see the misfortunes of our nation and of the sanctuary. But as his will in heaven may be, so he will do" (Macc 3:59).

The sun finally began to rise, putting an end to that longest of nights. With the rays of light on the horizon came Gorgias and his Greek soldiers, flooding the Jewish camp with swords and spears. But they found it empty.

Judas and his men had silently escaped their position in the night and rallied on the plain. Blowing the trumpet, the outnumbered Jewish contingent overwhelmed their unsuspecting Greek enemies. Victory belonged to Judas. Israel was saved.

Your long nights will eventually come to an end, too. The enemy on the horizon may still seem imposing when the sun rises. Hard feelings may still stand between you and your family members. The devil is still on the prowl, even when light covers the world anew.

Take heart, fellow soldier of the Lord. You do not head into battle alone. The same Lord who enabled a ragtag Jewish group to defeat a far greater force stands as your impenetrable shield.

The prophet Daniel saw Judas' struggles from his centuries-old vantage point. The sights and sounds of the prophecy frightened Daniel. Yet in love, the Lord gave Daniel a wonderful comfort at the beginning of this long, tumultuous vision. This comfort is meant for you as well, no matter what the morning brings...

Comfort for the Night

"Do not be afraid, Daniel, because from the first day that you began to commit your heart to gaining understanding and to humbling yourself before your God, your words have been heard, and I have come in response to your words" (Dan 10:12).

CHAPTER 29

Keeping Watch by Night

Luke 2:8-20

In 1697, Dutch sea captain, Willem de Vlamingh and his three ships had arrived at a river delta off of the West coast of Australia. Their mission was one of the utmost importance. They were looking for survivors of the *Ridderschap van Holland*, a ship that had gone missing two years earlier. Upon arriving at the previously unmapped river, De Vlamingh decided to have his ships split up into three groups in order to cover more ground. The tactic didn't work. De Vlamingh never found the *Ridderschap van Holland* or any of her survivors. He was about to turn back.

But traveling up that Australian river, De Vlamingh found something surprising. In fact, they had discovered the impossible. No one would believe their discovery back home—De Vlamingh and his men barely believed it themselves. Yet there it stood, right in front of them...a black swan.

For centuries Europeans had considered black swans an impossibility. In their world swans were always white. Knowing this, De Vlamingh and his men captured a couple of black swans to bring back home. The swans did not survive the arduous trip. Yet even in death, the very presence of those birds on the continent changed European minds forever.

De Vlamingh had inadvertently (yet quite literally) caused a "black swan event." He forced them to look upon a bird they thought had never existed. Ever since, people have used De Vlamingh's black swans to label any seemingly impossible event—especially those events that cause a major impact.

In his book *The Black Swan*, the statistician Nassim Nicholas Taleb sets the rules for what can constitute a "black swan event."[1] (He is the one who came up with the phrase, so I suppose he gets to set the terms of what constitutes a "Black Swan Event.") First, the event is a surprise—much like De Vlamingh's accidental discovery of the black swans themselves. Second, the event has a major effect—De Vlamingh's black swans forever changed European beliefs about their existence. Finally, the shocking discovery or the unexpected event is rationalized in hindsight. In De Vlamingh's case, we can almost hear their explanations on the ride home: "Well, when you think about it, of course black swans exist." Surprise...major ramifications... rationalization.

According to Taleb there have been multiple "black swan events" in our world: World War I, the rise of Hitler in Germany, the fall of the Soviet bloc, the terrorist attacks on 9/11. Each event surprised the world. Each event caused major changes to the world as we know it. And in each case, people continue to retroactively explain why we should have seen—even expected these "black swan events" from a mile away.

Should the shepherds have seen Jesus' birth coming? In Luke's beautiful chapter we see these poor men working the graveyard shift, watching their sheep under the dark night sky. Should they have known what was about to happen...and when...and where...and how...and why? Those shepherds witnessed the greatest even of their lives that night. They must have been kicking themselves in the days that followed: "How could we not see this wonderful event coming?"

Black swan events have a way of making us feel guilty like that. And that guilt can keep us up at night. "I should have known that sickness was coming for my father." "I should have been better prepared for when my ex hurt me." "Why didn't I see that other car swerving for me sooner?" Trying to rationalize the unforeseen can make us go crazy.

So, what should those shepherds have known leading up to the greatest night of their lives? Certainly, God had given his people a few key prophecies regarding the promised Messiah. Those shepherds

---

[1] Nassim Nicholas Taleb, *The Black Swan* (New York: Random House Trade Paperbacks, 2010), xxll.

probably knew that the coming Christ would come from the line of King David (2 Sam 7:12). They probably even knew that a Savior would be born in Bethlehem (Mic 5:2). And, most amazing of all, they may have even remembered that this coming Savior would be born of a virgin (Isa 7:14).

But there were so many other details those shepherds would have had no way of knowing. Who would have guessed just how humble the circumstances would be surrounding Jesus' birth? Even Jerusalem's greatest scholars would not have foreseen the hiddenness of God's arrival in flesh. The incarnation is a miracle so astounding, so unfathomable, and yet so personal that it might just be the greatest "black swan event" in the history of mankind.

Such an event needed to be announced. And here, once again, we are surprised by the first recipients of this greatest birth announcement. Why shepherds? Are they really the best delegation for the King of kings? Why not King Herod, the high priest, the Sanhedrin, the teachers of the law? Because our God loves to wrap his amazing "black swan events" in the swaddling clothes of humility.

There is no more humble profession than the night-watch shepherd. Under the stars they protect animals so weak that they cannot protect themselves. Over countless long nights they care for animals bound for sacrifice.

All at once their nightly routine changed forever. The brilliance of a multitude of angels dimmed the stars above. What a frightful sight! Any out-of-the-ordinary occurrence during the night made a shepherd's heart race. But this was something far more than any of them could have imagined. No wonder the first words from the heavens that night were words of comfort: "Do not be afraid" (Luke 2:10).

All fear could cease now. And on this night of nights the angels are quick to say why: "For behold, I bring you good news of great joy, which will be for all people: Today in the town of David, a Savior was born for you" (Luke 2:10-11). And just in case these shepherds missed the importance of the message, the angels emphatically proclaim who this Savior-child is: "He is Christ the Lord" (Luke 2:11).

Should they have seen this coming? The angels certainly did not expect them to know all of these details. In fact, they share every detail they can with these surprised shepherds. "You will find a baby wrapped in swaddling cloths and lying in a manger" (Luke 2:12). The angels could no longer contain their joy, singing God's highest praises even as God humbles himself in the lowliest of births.

Now the shepherds knew what was coming...and who had come. They quickly discuss the situation with each other. "Now let's go to Bethlehem and see this thing that has happened, which the Lord has made known to us" (Luke 2:15). In a rush, as fast as they could, they arrived at the stable and looked into the manger. There he was, Immanuel—God with us.

Finally, when they did pull themselves away from the nativity scene, those shepherds must have felt like De Vlamingh and his men. Who would believe the unfathomable sight they had seen? It didn't matter. They could no longer keep this good news to themselves. As stars gave way to sunlight, "They told others the message they had been told about this child" (Luke 2:17). And sure enough, even this greatest of all black swan events was met with wonder and amazement.

As our nights turn our thoughts to the past, guilt has a way of kicking us for past sins. Grief loves hindsight. It fuels our thoughts of "if only I had seen it coming." But we don't see everything coming. Even Mary and Joseph needed angels from the Lord to announce what was coming. Even shepherds at night needed an angel chorus to show them where the Savior was born.

You will not be able to know every event coming for you tonight or tomorrow or next year. But your Lord does. At just the right time he came among us, to die for you. Of course, he is going to see you through this night. And when the big events and unforeseen hardships come your way, remember the words announced by angels so many nights ago...

Comfort for the Night

"Do not be afraid. For behold, I bring you good news of great joy, which will be for all people: Today in the town of David, a Savior was born for you. He is Christ the Lord" (Luke 2:11).

CHAPTER 30

Flight by Night

Matthew 2:13-23

How much hardship do you let your children experience? A mother and father in the same home, raising the same children might answer that question differently. In fact, in my experience, mothers and fathers often disagree in their response to childhood hardship. Psychologists disagree, too. Some recommend removing every possible roadblock that stands in front of a child in order to give her the best possible life. Maybe you agree. But other psychologists, along with some parents, disagree. They maintain that some roadblocks are good for children to maneuver as they grow up—after all, how else can they prepare to maneuver the much larger roadblocks coming for them later in life?

The wall that stands between these two different parenting techniques is as ancient as parenting itself. Today, many call it a theory. Don't be fooled by its modern-sounding name. This theory has been around ever since Cain was born to Adam and Eve. It is called "positive disintegration." In a nutshell, the theory states that some roadblocks are good for children to maneuver as they learn how to cope with tension and anxiety.

Do you agree? I bet you do...to a certain extent. The difficulty comes when fathers and mothers stand at different points on the spectrum of allowable childhood difficulty. And the situation becomes even more challenging the more adults are involved. You and your spouse may be relatively close in how much allowable childhood difficulty you leave in front of your children. But what happens when grandma and grandpa stop by? What about the babysitter? Where does your child's teacher stand on "positive disintegration"? And perhaps most stressful of all—what do the other parents at the playground think about your approach to raising children?

I can't even imagine what it must have been like for Mary and Joseph. Not only were they first-time parents, they were raising someone else's child. They were raising the Son of God himself! They had to get this right. Forget the judging eyes of the other parents at the playground—God the Father was constantly watching from heaven.

If Joseph wasn't up at night worrying about all of these things he was certainly dreaming about them. New fathers tend to do that. But on this night, someone else entered his dream with a far more worrisome message. "Get up, take the child and his mother, and flee to Egypt" (Matt 2:13). Fear and anger must have welled up together in the naturally protective heart of this father, Joseph. The enemy was coming. It was time to go.

"Flee to Egypt" (Matt 2:13). With a toddler and a mother? How would this work? Joseph and his family had been in Bethlehem for quite some time. Couldn't they have received the warning with enough advanced notice to make the trip a comfortable one? Why the rush—was God the Father caught off guard?

I know those reactions sound like japes at God's expense, but new parents angrily ask questions like these. I am no longer a new parent and I still ask them. But Joseph never did. Instead, we simply read, like a sentence from a family scrapbook, "Joseph got up, took the child and his mother during the night, and left for Egypt" (Matt 2:14). Yet this was no sweet and simple vacation. Joseph and Mary fled with Jesus to escape murder. Many other innocent boys would not escape death in Bethlehem.

How many angry cries of fathers ascended up to heaven in the days that followed? How many tears of grief did the mothers of Bethlehem shed in the years that followed? How much guilt must have been felt by mothers and fathers—or even by soldiers—who felt the death of all of those children?

I know you feel guilt sometimes, too. If you have children then that guilt holds a special power over you. If you get this parenting thing wrong then it will be your child that suffers—perhaps for the rest of her life. Too many obstacles, or too many harsh words, and he will grow up an enemy of everyone—including you. Too few obstacles and the first little breeze of difficulty will blow her over so hard that she may never recover.

Psychologists can talk about the merits of "positive disintegration" all they want. But you are the one putting the theory into practical application on a daily basis. And I know, perhaps better even than you, that raising children often feels like a failing endeavor.

Is this what keeps you up a night? Isn't this the great fear of every parent—the one we never truly get past? What if I fail my children? Even great men like Noah and Samuel and David failed their children—some of them in spectacular fashion. What hope do we have?

Can I tell you what God your Father thinks about "positive disintegration"? As the perfect Parent, he can use even the heavy obstacles in your life for your good. We just don't always want to see these hardships from his perspective. Instead, we see them like our children see them—as experiences to be avoided.

Caught in the hubbub of night packing, overhearing the intense whispers of his earthly parents preparing for a long, unknown journey is a child. He isn't even named in the narrative, but he is the center of it all. We see him through the faithful eyes of his earthly father, Joseph. We get a glimpse of his precarious position through the pondering gaze of his mother, Mary. Yet in the middle of it all, the reason for the rush, the focal point of the murder, and the object of the soldiers' swords, remains Jesus.

His Father in heaven could have removed every obstacle for his beloved Son. But he didn't. In fact, there are times when it seems every possible hardship and obstruction is purposely placed in the path of the Savior. Bethlehem was merely the first of many. Nazareth would become just as dangerous…then so would Jerusalem.

God the Father walks his Son right into all of them. His reason for this, however, remains imminently different than our reasons for allowing obstacles for our children. The Father wasn't training his Son for earthly success. He was preparing his Son for death. The persecutions Jesus faced, the betrayal and the flogging, the cross he carried and his ultimate crucifixion remain more than just "positive disintegration." They are your justification. God the Father was thinking of his other children when he watched his Son die. His only-begotten Son had to give up his life in order to bring you into his family.

And that is only the beginning of your Father's love for you! He ever remains your perfect parent, working all things for your good. Sometimes, what you and I need to experience are joys. At other times hardship comes our way. Our Father allows these experiences as well. I'll let Peter explain why: "Now for a little while, if necessary, you have been grieved by various kinds of trials so that the proven character of your faith—which is more valuable than gold, which passes away even though it is tested by fire—may be found to result in praise, glory, and honor when Jesus Christ is revealed" (1 Pet 1:6-7).

You were brought into God's family for these very joys and hardships. So were your children. And now, like Joseph and Mary so many years ago, God may have given you children to take care of. Perhaps they are yours by birth. Maybe you adopted them into your family. Perhaps you have children entrusted to you as a teacher or neighbor. And the question might still keep you up at night: How can I raise these children faithfully—the way God wants me to raise them?

Can I offer you a loving reminder? You are just the right parent for those children to have. Notice I didn't say you are the "perfect" parent. You are the "right" parent. Your child is weird the way you were once weird (or the way your spouse was weird so many years ago). This child looks up to you. This child listens, even when it seems like he isn't listening. I can't tell you exactly which obstacles to allow and which to remove. And there will be days when you get it wrong and nights when you can't sleep.

Bring these concerns to your Father in prayer. He is ever listening. Then remember how he showed his love for you. Show that love for your children. Remind them that you also need to hear God's comforting promises when night falls…

Comfort for the Night

"The Lord is with me. I will not be afraid" (Ps 118:6).

CHAPTER 31

Twilight Teachings

John 3:1-21

A procession slowly pushed its way through the streets of an ancient Greek city. Somberly, pallbearers carried the coffin, the final resting chamber of the woman who had unexpectedly died. Past crashing waves and along coastal roads the group trudged staidly—the way people walk when they do not want to reach their destination. And this particular funeral had been especially heart-wrenching. Death had stolen away this young woman in the prime of her life.

Suddenly a cry rang out, breaking the silence. The pallbearers stopped. The crowd looked around. Ears bent, hoping to hear another cry. Sure enough, the cry sounded again. Curious eyes caught one another. This was the cry of an infant. But where was the baby? House doors were closed up. Not one mother or child stood on the sandy beach nearby. The confused pallbearers set down the casket.

The cry sounded forth again. Now everyone heard it clearly. This bawling was coming from *inside* the coffin! Quickly, carefully the men opened the box and found the source of the screams—a crying infant boy.

No one could ever remember hearing about such a miraculous event—even in their epic Greek stories. A pregnant mother gives birth in death? At her funeral? In her casket? And the child *lives*?

The baby born under these strangest of circumstances eventually survived to adulthood. In fact, he ascended to the most honorable seat of "Greek philosopher." His name was Gorgias of Epirus and all the greats of Greece looked up to him. It is said Gorgias influenced the famous doctor, Hippocrates. Thucydides, the father of scientific history, took some of his writing style from the sage of Epirus. The people of Delphi even erected a golden statue in honor of Gorgias.

Ironically, Gorgias didn't believe any of it existed. In fact, he didn't believe that anything really existed. And that nihilistic, nothing-really-exists perspective rested at the heart of the philosopher's world-view. Perhaps growing up without a family had jaded him. Maybe he understood just how impossible it feels to try and communicate your experiences to another person.

Personally, I think being born in death forever twisted Gorgias' world. How could he find meaning in a world that found his dead mother giving birth to him in her coffin? What possible hope could such a poor soul grasp a hold of?

One night in Jesus' ministry, a rich and powerful man snuck into the famous rabbi's presence—or at least he thought he had. No one else may have noticed him, but Jesus saw him coming from an eternity away. He knew Nicodemus by name. He understood that Nicodemus wanted to hear more. But Jesus also knew that Nicodemus needed the cover of darkness to hide him from his fellow Jewish rulers. And Jesus certainly knew how quickly those other Jewish rulers would turn on Nicodemus once they realized that the man he was talking with by the light of the moon was Jesus.

Nicodemus didn't know it yet, but he was walking into a funeral. And the Teacher in front of him was about to help Nicodemus climb into the casket. Of course, that was still coming. To start, let's get the introductions out of the way: "Rabbi, we know that you are a teacher who has come from God, for no one can do these miraculous signs you are doing unless God is with him" (John 3:2).

"We know" makes it sound like Nicodemus is speaking for the Sanhedrin. Perhaps he was representing a handful of secret believers in Judea's upper echelon. But Jesus didn't see Nicodemus coming from so far away to speak about other people. This nighttime class needed to be an intimate lesson—one that would both cut Israel's teacher to the core and heal his every wound.

"Amen, Amen, I tell you: Unless someone is born from above, he cannot see the kingdom of God" (John 3:3). Have you ever taught a lesson to someone? Have you ever wished to peer into the mind of your child or grandchild? Ever wonder what your Sunday school students are really struggling with? Wouldn't it be nice to see into a person's heart like Jesus does? Jesus knew exactly what Nicodemus needed to hear...even if he didn't want to hear it at first.

"Nicodemus, you need to be born again." Nicodemus responds, "How can a man be born when he is old?" (John 3:4). Can we forgive the confused man for his reply? This wasn't a physical rebirth Jesus was talking about—at least, not like the birth that originally brought us into the world. No, this rebirth would require "water and the Spirit" (John 3:5).

Do you remember why? Your first birth into this world was exactly like Nicodemus' birth. In fact, it was just like Gorgias' birth. You were born in death. It might as well have been a funeral. "Whatever is born of the flesh is flesh." Jesus is talking about the sinful flesh that wraps around you and inside of you. Maybe that reminder makes all of us nihilists by nature. Maybe there is a part of us that wants to believe that nothing really exists. After all, thinking of everything as if it were nothing helps me not to worry about anything. But Jesus did not come into this world to make you a cold, hopeless nihilist. You may have been born in death like Gorgias, but you are not bound to his casket forever.

"You are the teacher of Israel...and you do not know these things?" (John 3:10). Nicodemus didn't understand. But Jesus did. Beneath night's shadow the Light of the world shone into the heart of this confused Jew. "If I have told you earthly things and you do not believe, how will you believe if I tell you heavenly things?" (John 3:12). How indeed?

But we all struggle with the cynicism that death brings. What's the point of believing in a heaven if this world so often feels like hell? Can I keep eternal life in the forefront amidst a world filled with death? And since we have been born in sinful flesh, what hope do we have?

Jesus brings up an Old Testament account that Nicodemus finally did know. Whether Jesus was still speaking these words of the chapter to Nicodemus or his disciples, in the end they are meant for everyone. A long time ago, when the poisonous venom of death surrounded the angry Israelites in the wilderness, Moses lifted up a bronze serpent. It represented another moment of grace from their Lord—a specter of undeserved love standing above an indignant nation.

Just when God's people most deserved death, he gave them life. Everyone who looked upon the snake in faith was miraculously healed. It all pointed ahead to Jesus. "The Son of Man must be lifted up, so that everyone who believes in him shall not perish but have eternal life" (John 3:14-15). That faith comes through rebirth. That rebirth comes through God's word and baptism.

The Apostle Paul makes the connection better than I ever could. "We were therefore buried with him by this baptism into his death, so that just as he was raised from the dead through the glory of the Father, we too would also walk in a new life" (Rom 6:4). Born in a casket of death, you were reborn through the waters of your baptism. That cleansing flood washed away your sin. It placed faith in your heart. On that day a throne was erected in you, a seat from where your loving Lord can reign in your life.

And because of Jesus' death and resurrection, that's what you have now—life. It is the truth of this midnight lesson we are sharing together. This is the lesson you get to teach to your children and grandchildren. Your life is not hopeless. You have existence. You are loved. And you have a future, a glorious eternity for which you were reborn...

Comfort for the Night

"To those who believe in his name, he gave the right to become children of God. They were born, not of blood, or of the desire of the flesh, or of a husband's will, but born of God" (John 1:12-13).

CHAPTER 32

Haunted Waters

Matthew 14:22-33

Perched above the River Thames in the shadow of London's Tower Bridge sits an ancient and imposing structure. She has stood in the city longer than most of the other buildings. In fact, she is nearly a thousand years old—although don't tell her that. She still appears regal, standing among London's most awe-inspiring locations.

She is the Tower of London and Londoners have made use of her in a variety of ways. She has served as an armory, a treasury, and a menagerie. She was once the home of the Royal Mint. She has been a public record office. She has housed the empire's most precious artifacts as well as her most notorious criminals.

Like any prominent English woman, the Tower of London is at once stately and ominous, regal and riveting. She has held some of the most important people in English history, from Sir Walter Raleigh to Queen Elizabeth. Even as recently as 1952, she kept the murderous Kray twins locked away.

Intriguing, imposing, striking; the Tower of London is many things. But most of all, she is haunted. As any Englishman can tell you, the Kray twins were *not* her last residents. The Tower continues to house perhaps the saddest woman in English history. You can see her, if you like—the beheaded Anne Boleyn. A hundred-year-old song explains the sight some still see to this day:

She walks the Bloody Tower!
With her head tucked underneath her arm
At the midnight hour...

She comes to haunt King Henry.[1]

Hidden away in the Tower of London Anne Boleyn walks silently, holding her severed head under her arm. Weeping can be heard as she moves along.

What is it about Anne Boleyn that draws so many to her? Was it her betrayal at the hands of her husband, the merciless King Henry VIII? Does she appeal to some sort of "everyman" spirit that opposes a powerful monarchy? Perhaps. But I think it is simpler than that. People just like a good ghost story. That is, we like hearing about ghosts and hauntings until we actually come face to face with them. Stories that enthrall during the day can frighten us to death at night. Are you picturing Anne Boleyn by the light of day? No problem then. But wait until tonight. You might just see her everywhere—walking outside your window, hovering around the corners of your house, in the movements of your children getting a drink of water during the night.

Our imaginations hold such power over us. Under the dark of night, anything can seem real. Every "what if" becomes "but when."

It seemed every possible "what if" was coming to fruition for the disciples one night on the waves of the Sea of Galilee. Jesus had sent them on ahead of him. He needed time alone to pray. The waves beat against the boat. Some of these disciples had grown up sailing these waters. They knew them as well as any fisherman. Yet even Peter and Andrew, James and John could not control their boat against such fierce wind and pounding waves.

Seeing death in the water, those beleaguered disciples didn't think their circumstances could get any worse. Then they saw a ghost. The cried out, the way children do when something so terrible, so otherworldly stands before them. "It's a ghost!" (Matt 14:26).

Could it have been? Do apparitions and ghouls really exist? The disciples seemed to think so. Of course, anything seems possible when darkness surrounds us and death seems imminent. Anything, that is...except Jesus.

Why are we so quick to believe in the fantastical—ghosts, aliens, zombies—in the lonely darkness, but so very slow to remember that

---

[1] *Catalog of Copyright Entries Part 3*, Vol. 30, No. 1 (Washington DC: Government Printing Office, 1936), 2350.

our Jesus is real? Why does fear unravel faith, and how can it do it so quickly?

You know the answer by now. Each of us has a sinful nature that, under the cover of darkness and in the midst of fear, jumps headlong into doubt and worry. Every "what if" becomes possible, even this one: "What if God left me to this eerie emptiness on purpose?"

Had there been time to think among the rigging in the middle of the wind storm, some of those men might have dared to remember that it was Jesus himself who sent them on ahead into this situation. In fact, "Jesus urged the disciples to get into the boat and to go ahead of him to the other side" (Matt 14:22).

Is the Lord responsible for the fright that overwhelms you? Does he know what you are going through? Has he left you to the monstrous devices of your world, your enemies...or even your imagination?

The ghostly figure moved along the water. It was uninhibited by the bellowing wind and the crashing waves. It walked near the boat. Frozen, the disciples neither called out to the ghoulish phantasm, nor did they cry out for their Savior. The figure began to pass by.

"It's a ghost!" (Matt 14:26).

It wasn't though. And once again, the voice of their master, the call of the King of the universe echoed off the Galilean waters to silence wind, stop waves, and calm troubled hearts. "Take heart! It is I! Do not be afraid" (Matt 14:27).

Immediately, the ghost they couldn't get away from became their Lord they couldn't get close enough to. As always, Peter led the way. Armed with a newfound courage, Peter cried out, "Lord, if it is you, command me to come to you on the water" (Matt 14:28).

Knowing what would happen from before the creation of the world, Jesus bid Peter, "Come!" (Matt 14:29). Peter's first few steps were nothing short of miraculous. His next few strides became uncertain. His final steps appeared to be his last. The heart that saw death in the wind and waves, that then witnessed the ghostly figure, that became bold enough to walk on water, now fell apart all over again.

His logical mind assessed his miraculous situation. *People don't walk on water!* Peter's mind raced. *What am I doing?* And we've been there, too. The wind and waves of our lives, the storms and ghoulish-looking apparitions bash our faith into doubt. What's left for us in moments like these? A fear of anything and everything? The "what ifs" becomes "but whens."

And our cry rings out in the darkness of our long night, "Lord, save me!" (Matt 14:30).

And he does. Jesus stretches his hand out—the very hand that created you, the hand that kept every enemy at bay, the hand that bears the nail marks of your salvation—and saves you. The apparitions disappear. Fear fades away. And a warning comes, "You of little faith, why did you doubt?" (Matt 14:31).

Why indeed? Even the most stalwart believers wrestle with doubts and fears. And we are not always the most stalwart. We need to hear the powerful, calming, guiding words of our Savior.

So, hear them once again, even as the waves wash over you and the wind howls. No ghost exists. Anne Boleyn does not walk around in dark, forbidding towers. No enemy can overcome you. Even demons scurry away at the voice of your risen Savior. And now, in the gloom he speaks to your lonely, beleaguered heart with his ever-powerful promise...

Comfort for the Night

"Take heart! It is I! Do not be afraid" (Matt 14:27).

CHAPTER 33

Silence

Luke 22:3-6

What aspect of Jesus' ministry tells us the most about him? Some would say his miracles. Certainly those acts of power—healing the sick, driving out demons and raising the dead —reveal Jesus to be more than a mere man. Others point to Jesus' words. The people who originally listened to his lessons had to admit that Jesus taught with an authority unlike any of their teachers of the law.

Those are all accurate answers. Jesus' miracles and his teachings always pointed to who he is. But perhaps there is another key aspect of his ministry that tells us just as much. Jesus preached not only with words, but with silence. In fact, those moments when the Lord chose to be silent might just be the most poignant moments in his entire ministry.

When his own hometown of Nazareth rose up and tried to throw him off the nearby cliff, Jesus silently walked through them. After that, Jesus remained relatively silent towards those he grew up with. Or what about the time in the courtyard when Peter denied that he knew Jesus? There was no sermon from the Savior. No rebuttal sounded forth from his nighttime court. Jesus simply looked at Peter with a silent stare. Christ's glance said more than any word ever could.

On this Wednesday of Holy Week, we see Jesus envelope himself within that all-important silence. But where is he? Who is he with? Not one of the Gospels tells us. All we hear happening on this Wednesday are the words of everyone else. Judas Iscariot speaks with the chief priests. Together they talk about their plot of betrayal against Jesus. Everyone is delighted. Even Satan is busy whispering, convincing Judas to enact his betrayal and capture that ultimately leads to Jesus' crucifixion.

But the Lord remains silent. So does Scripture. God does not tell us where Jesus was or what he was doing. Was he alone, taking time for prayer and meditation on his word? Was he with others, teaching men and women the lessons we heard from earlier days? Perhaps Jesus silently prepared himself for what was coming. And make no mistake, a lot was coming. The next day would bring the joy of celebrating—and fulfilling—the final Passover. That night Judas and the high priest would fulfill their plans of betrayal and capture. The long night that followed would see Jesus before the Sanhedrin. The next morning would place Jesus before Pontius Pilate. Whips that now quietly hung on the walls of the Roman barracks, would soon dance across the back of the Son of God. Unspeakable torment silently approached.

Everything would culminate at the cross. Physical pain and anguish would give way to the eternal agony of hell. All of it thrust upon Jesus as he suffered away the punishment meant for the entire world. With all of this in mind, in the middle of this Holy Week, perhaps Jesus needed this silence.

Did King David see this silence coming? Throughout his psalms David writes about the coming Messiah and the suffering he would endure. Psalm 22 reads as a veritable blow-for-blow account of what awaited the promised Messiah on the cross. And if David saw every strike, every agony coming for his perfect descendant, then it seems he also noticed the silence that would precede it.

If Psalm 22 prophesies the grief of Good Friday, then Psalm 39 sends us into the quiet of Jesus' silent Wednesday. "I will guard my ways so that I do not sin with my tongue" (Ps 39:1). Even as the crowds cheered Jesus' entrance into Jerusalem on Palm Sunday, as his enemies tried to trap him in his words on Tuesday, and when the mob captured and beat him, the Lamb of God remained silent. "I will keep a muzzle on my mouth as long as the wicked are confronting me" (Ps 39:1).

But even on Wednesday, perhaps *especially* in the silence of this day, Jesus fulfills David's words. "Lord, help me understand my end" (Ps 39:4). David rightly used those words to consider the eternal hell his sins had earned him. In such grim circumstances life seemed meaningless. "My brief time before you is like nothing. Indeed, every person, even at his best, is just a puff of air. A man flickers like a mirage. He really has no more effect than a breeze" (Ps 39:5-6). And while that is true of every sinner—including us—it is not true of great David's greater Son, Jesus.

On this silent Wednesday, Jesus seems to be considering both the end of his ministry and the culmination of every Messianic prophecy. David said of himself, "See, you have cut short my days" (Ps 39:5). But Jesus defined it. Jesus *fulfilled* it.

The weight of the world pressed hard against the Lord on Wednesday. And in these moments, when the calm silences the world before the storm, the big picture comes into view. Names and faces pass through the mind's eye. Jesus could picture Adam and Eve in the garden; their murderous son, Cain; the world under water as Noah's family floated above; Abraham's worries and King David's sinful desires.

And there, in that silence, Jesus could remember you. He could remember you as his *why* and *reason* for approaching the cross. He could think ahead to all of your moments of silent guilt and quiet agony. He could remember your future hatreds and desires and worries. They could all flash before his eyes—every single one of them—so that he could suffer them all away on your cross.

Such is the power of silence. It grabs us and holds us tight. We yearn for silence when we do not have it, and break apart under its weight when we finally find it. Silence pauses our world, but then makes our minds race. It brings new possibilities, but always recalls the most painful memories.

Listen to how David used his silence. "Hear my prayer, O Lord. Listen to my cry" (Ps 39:12). Jesus did hear David's prayer. That was why he took on the silence of this Wednesday. It is why he silenced himself on Good Friday. And it is why God the Father remained silent at Calvary. Like David, Jesus cried out to his Father, but no word came. Nothing sounded back in reply.

Jesus took that eternal silence upon himself so that you would never experience it. The Son of God stood between his Father's punishment and you. And now he sits between you and your loving Father in heaven. He remains silent so that he can always listen to your every worry, and your every joy.

And then the Savior who was so very silent on that Wednesday of long ago…*answers.*

Make time for those moments of silence in your life. Push away the world for a moment in order to listen to your Savior's words in Scripture. That's where he speaks to you. That's where he shows you the full extent of his love. And those are the words that guide you in responding to him with your words, your prayers.

He promises to help you understand your end. And because of Jesus, your end is really just your beginning. The silence of your death will give way to the perfect sounds of your eternal life…where your Savior is silently, patiently waiting for you.

Comfort for the Night

"The Lord is my shepherd. I lack nothing. He causes me to lie down in green pastures. He leads me beside quiet waters. He restores my soul" (Ps 23:1-3).

CHAPTER 34

Dark Gethsemane

Luke 22:39-46

"Why is this night different from all the other nights?" The question rang throughout the upper room. Upon hearing it, Jesus must have smiled. This was the age-old phrase designated for the youngest child to ask at the Passover meal. That question meant something more on this particular night, for this particular Passover celebration.

So why was this night different from all the other nights? Let me count the ways.

This night marked the final celebration of that ancient Passover ordinance. No longer would lambs need to be sacrificed. Never again would cups and bitter herbs and unleavened bread need to be placed and consumed in just the right order. Tomorrow this Old Testament shadow would see its long-awaited fulfillment.

This night marked the first celebration of a new meal, a meal founded on Jesus' *new* covenant. The unleavened bread once reserved for the Passover meal would now be Jesus' real body given for believers. The wine once set aside for drinking at just the right time in the old meal would now be poured out as Jesus' blood for the forgiveness of sins.

So many moving forces made this night different every other night. The Lord would be betrayed. The disciples would abandon him. Enemy forces would finally capture the one they had plotted against for so long.

Could this night have been any *more* different from every other night? Even for the Lord, the events of this evening diverged from any prior night he experienced. Perhaps he thought about each of those differences headed for him as he listened to the question. Why is this night different from all the other nights? This night would begin the Son of Man's long road of suffering and anguish, of hell and death. This evening would mark the Savior's sweat beading down his brow, dripping like drops of blood onto the ground.

On this one night darkness would be allowed to reign.

So many believers have experienced their longest, darkest nights throughout the ages. Now after hearing the origins of darkness and the beginnings of sin, after sitting with Abraham under the stars and watching Jacob wrestle with God, having witnessed night fall on prophets and kings and warriors and shepherds, we have finally arrived at the longest night of them all.

Why is this night different from all the other nights? Only Jesus knew. He had perfectly explained the intricate details of this night on multiple occasions to his disciples. "The Son of Man must suffer many things; be rejected by the elders, the chief priests, and the experts in the law; be killed." Jesus even explained the culmination of all of his upcoming suffering, that he would "after three days rise again" (Mark 8:31).

At first Peter vowed to stop it. In reply, Jesus pointed out how disastrous Peter's good intentions really were: "Get behind me, Satan! You do not have your mind set on the things of God, but the things of men" (Mark 8:33). Then to a man, Jesus' closest companions shrugged it off. They had been given the blueprints to the oncoming destruction by the very Architect of the universe, and they still didn't see the enormity of the night ahead.

The ancient Passover questions had been asked for the last time. The meal ended. Then Jesus and his disciples sang a hymn. It was probably one of the psalms assigned for that very purpose on that very night. Having already read Psalm 113 and Psalm 114, they might have sung Psalms 115-118.

"Under pressure I cried to the Lord" (Ps 118:5). Jesus sang the words as he walked with his disciples into the darkness of the night. "The Lord is with me. I will not be afraid" (Ps 118:6). Jesus knew that those words would always be true every day of a believer's life... except tomorrow. Tomorrow, Good Friday, his Father would have to abandon him to the hell that should have been ours. "All the nations surrounded me…They surrounded me, yes, they surrounded me" (Ps 118:11).

Perhaps Jesus even sang with his disciples, "The Lord has chastened me severely" (Ps 118:18). That was coming, too. In fact, his severe suffering was almost here. He entered the quiet of the Garden of Gethsemane.

But the promised Messiah had given himself a little time. Orchestrated from the beginning of all things, Jesus allowed himself moments of prayer to his Father in heaven. In a garden he would bear his human heart in raw, uncensored pleas.

We don't expect to see Jesus this way—even on this night. His disciples must have been as surprised to see the anguish as we are to hear it. The Lord of heaven and earth says, "My soul is overwhelmed with sorrow, even to the point of death. Stay here and keep watch" (Mark 14:34). The disciples fell asleep. It had been a long day. The Passover meal had ended. They must have yearned for bed.

Jesus would never sleep again. He fell on the ground in prayer. "Father, if you are willing, take this cup away from me" (Luke 22:42). Does your Savior's prayerful request frighten you? It frightens me. What if the Father had been willing to take the cup of suffering away from his Son? Wouldn't that mean an eternity of suffering would pour out on us?

Why is this night different from all the other nights? Perhaps what makes this night different is the gospel writers' clear look at Jesus' humanity. There is no sin in Jesus' request, yet he looks so exposed. An angel attends Jesus. The night continues on. Darkness reigns.

Jesus faces every grueling temptation as a man. He continues his perfect course as God. He knew his Father's will. There was never a chance that his cup of suffering would ever become our cup of suffering. That's why Jesus prayed those all important words, "Nevertheless, not my will, but yours be done" (Luke 22:42).

Jesus knew the betrayer was on his way. The time he had set aside for prayer was coming to a close. Amidst blood-like drops of sweat he prayed to his Father one final time. Jesus poured out his heart to his Father. His Father poured out suffering on Jesus.

The time in the Garden was ending. The betrayer had arrived. And Jesus walked right up to him. He had lost Judas, who came to betray his Lord with a kiss. Jesus would soon lose the rest of his disciples too.

In a matter of hours the trials and the angry cries and the scourging and the wooden cross would all be thrust upon him. It had to be this way. This was the night when darkness reigned.

So why is this night different from all the other nights? Because Jesus took this night from you. Never will you sleeplessly spend a night that precedes your eternal suffering. Jesus took all of it upon himself. You will not face hell tomorrow...or next week...or ever.

Jesus sang about that very fact with you in mind. As he walked to his place of prayer, as he prepared his heart to take your place in hell, he looked even further ahead. He saw you on Easter Sunday through the opening of an empty tomb. He witnessed your sure and certain eternity with him in heaven forever.

Even on that darkest of nights, Jesus sang your salvation...

Comfort for the Night

"I will not die. No, I will live" (Ps 118:17).

CHAPTER 35

A Watery Grave

Matthew 27:57-66

A Greek farmer was walking through a dark field. His hands passed silently over the tall grass. The grass reminded him of the grounds around his family farm. He had led horses in his childhood through fields like this one. He recalled lifting his little girl atop one of those horses, the way his father once lifted him. Her smiling face let out a squeal of joy as the horse started to trot away down the path.

The farmer's eyes now scanned the horizon. They caught a glimpse of the mountains in the distance, rising high above the grasslands he now silently stepped through. High, imposing rock walls prompted thoughts of the walks he and his wife took to the nearby town. Every year they would carry a portion of their harvest along narrow mountain passes. The roads could be treacherous, but seeing the love of his life aboard their wagon made him feel stronger.

The farmer enjoyed bringing up those memories, the way you and I page through a scrapbook or glance at framed photos on our grandparents' walls. He treasured those moments.

That's when the farmer met a river. He looked down at the calm rush of water. He needed a drink. The walk had tired him more than he realized. He needed to cross the river. He needed to keep on moving. But first he had to get a drink.

His cupped hand plunged into the cool, flowing water. Lifting it to his mouth he tasted the refreshing water. Never before had water satisfied him like this. He cupped his hand again and again, drinking as much water as he could. It tasted so good.

Then he paused. Glancing at the grass he passed his hand through again. That grass, it reminded him of…something. He looked up at those imposing mountains in the distance, across the river. He used to pass through mountains like those…with someone. He needed to get going. But where was he going again?

One more drink. Then he needed to be off. He had a long journey yet. He had to get…*somewhere.*

That Greek farmer didn't know it, but he was walking through the depths of the afterlife. His long journey through life had now led him into death—to a river that every Greek person believed they would one-day reach. It was the river Lethe: the "stream of forgetfulness." According to his Greek faith, every person who died had to drink from the river and forget everything: the places they lived, the memories they treasured, even the people they loved. Then they could be reincarnated. They could hope to live again.

Aren't you glad that isn't how it works? Imagine walking in some ominous afterlife, reaching a river you have to drink from, and slowly forgetting all of your memories! If Oscar Wilde was right, and "Memory…is the diary that we all carry about with us,"[1] then the Greeks believed that death ripped that diary out of your hands.

You can see what that Greek legend was getting at. Rivers are the world's great memory-wipes. Whatever their watery banks get a hold of washes away forever. Sometimes that's exactly what we're looking for.

If only I could turn the water on during the night and wash away all of those guilty thoughts that pass through my mind. That word I said to my brother so many years ago; the thing I stole that I can no longer give back; that family gathering I refused to attend and wish I had. Those dark sins that creep up under the cover of darkness dance through our minds. If only we could forget them. If only we could wash them away.

Could flowing streams ever wash away the horrific memories of Good Friday? Many wished they could. Peter may have wished he could drink from some eternal stream in order to forget his sins of denial. Judas must have yearned for water that could wash away his

---

[1] Oscar Wilde, *The Importance of Being Earnest* (New York: Dover Publications, Inc., 2008), 22.

betrayal. When he was unable to find it, he took matters into his own hands. Perhaps even Mary yearned for the clear washing away of her memory as the sword of her Son's death pierced her own soul, too.

But the dark, foreboding waters of the Lethe do not flow through Jerusalem. The awful memories remained, forever carved into the hearts of those who witnessed it. Their Teacher, their Lord, the Son of God was dead.

After the screams of crucifixion fell to silence and after the shocked crowds dispersed, two forgotten souls stepped forward. Joseph of Arimathea and Nicodemus, two men hidden among the angry leaders and shouting crowds, boldly asked for the lifeless body of the Christ. With hushed haste, Joseph cleaned Jesus' mangled body. Wet with water, sinful hands washed dried blood off of the Son of God.

If only a powerful stream could blast through the carved tomb to wash away the horrors of the day. If only the flowing tears of the women standing opposite the tomb could erase their memories of this darkest of Fridays. Could the diary of this day be buried with their loved one in the tomb forever?

No streams could wash away the truths of that day. Jesus had died. The River Lethe was nowhere to be found. The tomb remained dry. Or did it?

Deep among the hewn rocks of that new tomb, just before the stone was rolled in front, the Lord pulled you in. Waters bubbled around the opening. A rising tide inundated the silent sepulcher. And you washed into the grave of the Lord.

This isn't the frightening scene of a horror novel. This watery tomb is your salvation. These aren't the waters of the River Lethe. This is the flood of your baptism. Those waters wash you right in to the tomb of your Savior. They bury you behind that stone. They surround you in rock. They submerge you in water that bears the name of your Triune God.

Your baptismal waters carrying you through Jesus' tomb are waters of forgetfulness. They intrinsically connect you to the eternal promise of your Savior: "I will forgive their guilt, and I will remember their sins no more" (Jer 31:34). They wash you clean before your heavenly Father.

Those baptismal waters *resurrect* you. Listen as the Apostle Paul makes one of the most hauntingly beautiful connections in Scripture: "We were therefore buried with [Jesus] by this baptism into his death, so that just as he was raised from the dead through the glory of the Father, we too would also walk in a new life" (Rom 6:4). And if those waters of your baptism rushed you into Jesus' tomb, Jesus himself carries you out on Easter Sunday.

I write these words in the throes of a COVID epidemic. Remember those dark days? Tears fell over countless caskets holding loved ones they wish they could have back. Many passed away in empty hospital rooms while moms and dads, sons and daughters longingly waited outside. Death hung heavy over every aspect of life. Tombs filled up.

There are times when God purposefully draws death before our eyes. And we often need the reminder. All things perish. Every thing and everyone that is alive will eventually die.

But you died already. Your baptism washed you into Christ's tomb. Your sins, your guilt, your worries, your anger all washed away. Your sinful self died, and you were made alive. The death at your baptism drained the power and sting of any other death that hangs over you. Jesus, the Lord of the "River of Sins Forgotten" has you drink deep from the well of his salvation. Life is yours.

Forevermore.

Comfort for the Night

"He will wipe away every tear from their eyes, and death shall be no more" (Rev 21:4).[2]

---

[2] Concordia Publishing House, *The Lutheran Study Bible, English Standard Version* (Saint Louis: Concordia Publishing House, 2009), 2233.

CHAPTER 36

Peter's Prison

Acts 12:1-11

Many lost their heads to the guillotine in Halifax, Yorkshire over the years. The frightening death-device towered over guilty souls and innocent spectators alike. The punishment might have appeared brutal, but at least it was quick.

By 1623, many cities used the guillotine to enact the death penalty. What distinguished Halifax from the rest of them was an interesting loophole. Their law included, quite literally, an "escape clause." If a person could pull his head out precisely before the blade came down on his neck, and if he successfully evaded the police and escaped the city, he would be free. But there was a catch. The man who successfully avoided the blade and outran the guards could never enter the town again.

Against all odds, one lucky man was able to do just that. Awaiting the cutting slice of the blade on his day of execution, John Lacy successfully pulled his head out just in time. He evaded the authorities and left the city in exile. However, he misunderstood his rights as a fugitive. He thought "forever" meant "a few years." And so, seven years after his narrow escape from death, John Lacy returned to town. The authorities captured him all over again, sentenced him to the guillotine...where he wasn't so lucky the second time.

John Lacy had escaped death, only to return into its clutches.

In the early days of the Church, believers must have been wondering if bars and locks would be their inevitable future. Swiftly, King Herod, the grandson of Herod the Great, began acting like his grandfather. He mistreated followers of Jesus. He had John's brother, James, sentenced to death with the sword. Then came the centerpiece of all of this persecution. During a festival, Herod finally caught Peter—the unofficial leader of this new group of Christians. And no one would be able to take away Herod's new possession. Four squads of four soldiers each watched over Peter as he silently sat behind bars.

Whether Peter knew Herod's plan for him or not, he must have noticed a pattern. A preacher of grace was captured, about to stand trial before the Jews in Jerusalem, around the Passover. Men on death row think about such things during their long, lonely nights. Perhaps one of Jesus' final conversations with Peter stuck in the disciple's mind that evening. After the risen Lord patiently, lovingly reinstated Peter he pointed him to the day he would die—and the way he would die. "When you are old, you will stretch out your hands, and some-one else will tie you and carry you where you do not want to go" (John 21:18).

Would you ever forget a prediction of your death? How could you—especially when death seems imminent? How could Peter not carefully think through every word Jesus said on that day? Wouldn't he wonder if "when you are old" was how he felt at that moment? King Herod's soldiers were now tying up their prisoner and telling him where to go.

Were these Peter's final moments on earth? His close friend James already met the sword and was now with the Lord. Was Peter next?

Are you next? I bet you have considered the question at least once during your long nights of trouble here on earth. Are these the final moments of my life? Maybe the thought haunts your mind even now.

The devil creeps in with those thoughts, too. When it seems as though the end is in sight, when your life may in fact be coming to a close, that Prince of lies arrives with his most dangerous temptations of all. He gets your heart to ask: "Have I done enough?" He sends down the gauntlet of wonder and doubt in a moment when we cry out for certainty. And even if we are resolved to look to Christ—as we should!—the devil has us view the Lord as the implacable Judge of all, waiting to doom us to eternal destruction in hell.

Is this why we try so very hard to keep ourselves busy? The moment we are forced the sit still, the dark cloud of these worries and anxieties hovers over us. Each night brings a new cavalcade of fears and disasters. Every day feels like it could—or should—be our last one on earth. And instead of welcoming the end, we hear that nagging question all over again: "Have I done enough?"

Do you remember the answer to that? It is a pretty simple, "No, you haven't done enough." No amount of good works can save you. That list of accomplishments you wrote out for your obituary some-day? It could go on for pages and pages, and still it wouldn't be enough to earn a joy filled future. The situation is far worse than the devil and your sinful nature makes it out to be.

The devil must have paraded each sinful memory before Peter that night in prison. If he could get Peter to doubt God's love, if he could get Peter to despair—like he did with Judas Iscariot—then the ancient enemy of God would declare another victory.

What a struggle for a believer as the night grows ever longer! And make no mistake, every believer wrestles with these thoughts of "have I done enough." Many years later, Peter wrote to believers experiencing some of the same persecutions he suffered. Listen to his beautiful encouragements: "You rejoice very much, even though now for a little while, if necessary, you have been grieved by various kinds of trials" (1 Pet 1:6).

It would have been easy to forget that as death hung in the air of that prison cell. But then, seemingly out of nowhere, light flooded Peter's room. A voice rang out, "Quick, get up!" (Acts 12:7). Chains miraculously fell off Peter's wrists. The angel led Peter right out of prison, passed sleeping guards and through iron gates.

It all seemed like a dream as Peter walked with the angel down the middle of the road under the nighttime stars. But then the angel left Peter's sight. All at once he realized this was no dream at all. "Now I know for sure that the Lord sent his angel and rescued me from the hand of Herod" (Acts 12: This was not to be Peter's last night on earth. The Lord still had work for his disciple to carry out.

I don't know what hangs over your head. Perhaps death really does feel imminent. Maybe you are facing punishment for something you did...or for something you didn't do. Perhaps you wait for the clarity that only tomorrow's sun can bring.

Guillotines may still glint in the sun. But as you stare down even that kind of death, please remember that you have avoided the worst death of all. It took something far greater than a quick pull of the head and an action far more selfless than outrunning local police. Your eternal salvation was won by your Savior who walked straight into death. He could have escaped it at any moment, but he remained steadfast in fulfilling his promise to save you.

Don't run back to your doubts and fears. Shut up the voice that questions your sure forgiveness in Jesus. No more "but have I done enough?" Here's what Jesus did for you. And don't be afraid, because it is everything and more…

Comfort for the Night

"He gave us a new birth into a living hope through the resurrection of Jesus Christ from the dead, into an inheritance that is undying, undefiled, and unfading, kept in heaven for you" (1 Pet 1:3-4).

Chapter 37

A Blade Turned Inward

Acts 16:16-34

Rivers crisscrossed through the town where I grew up. It seemed like no matter where I walked bridges traversed my path. For most of the residents the various waterways added to the serenity of the area, which someone long ago nicknamed "The Little Yellowstone."

I hated it. I was deathly afraid of deep water. And while my childhood friends and I would swim through many of the smaller streams, I held my breath whenever we drove across the deep rivers. Something about that dark, watery abyss always sent shivers down my spine.

One bridge in particular frightened me the most. An imposing dam still rests underneath it. One side holds a manmade lake. On the other side, the river cuts through the steep, jagged rock.

I just recently stopped crossing that bridge in my nightmares (even though I've been an adult for quite some time now). I think I finally know why that particular bridge continues to hold such a dark spell on me. One day in grade school, one of my friends told me that a woman had walked to the middle of the bridge and jumped off onto the rocks below. I remember asking why someone would do that. He said she did it to die.

My town wasn't that big. She was someone I remembered seeing. I could picture her face. I just couldn't imagine why she would purposefully throw her body off that bridge. She had a husband. She was a mother who had children at home.

I think about her a lot. What was it like to slowly walk to the edge of that bridge while steady traffic passed beside her? What thoughts ran through her mind as she took her final steps? Was she committed to the act once she looked down on the rocks? Who did she think about when she stood on the edge of the railing? Did she have time to repent in the milliseconds before her death? Did God understand the storm in her soul? Could he forgive that hurricane? Did she even want that forgiveness?

Round and round my thoughts wrap around that moment in time. It is almost like I'm standing there next to her. And what if I was there on that bridge standing beside her? What words could possibly stop her?

After years and years of thought, my sinful mind has only been able to bring me to one conclusion. I wouldn't know what to say—not right away. I don't know if I could physically stop her. But after years of strife—the type of strife I know you, too, have endured as a sinner—the one, dark epiphany I've reached is *why* she would jump off.

Can I share that with you? I've been on that bridge. My eyes have scanned the rocks below. My mind has considered the oblivion beyond.

Have you stood on that bridge? Be honest. I know it hurts to think about. In fact, I know it hurts a lot to think about. Your world has collapsed in on you, leaving you crumpled up like a used tissue. You feel as though you aren't good for anything or anyone. Was it someone you deeply loved who betrayed you to this lonely precipice? Perhaps you feel as though you are used up. Or maybe you are surrounded. You see no way out.

A jailer once stood on that bridge with you. He couldn't see passed his own predicament. The scene was dark. The circumstances appeared more than unlucky. A freak earthquake left the entire building standing, but opened every single cell he guarded. If only the roof had fallen! At least he could end his life at his post—a proud, loyal Roman guard—the victim of the most random of tragedies. No one would look down on his family. The city could name the jail after him.

But not like this. The ground was still now. The cells open. The room that just moments earlier echoed with the hymns of the two newest prisoners now fell eerily silent. Everyone was gone.

If only the jailor was, too.

At precisely these moments of darkness the devil rushes in. He sees the lonely sheep separated from the rest of the flock. No shepherd is in sight. Doubt comes in.

He leaves only one escape option: suicide. Like the most dastardly of conquering commanders, the devil pounds this poor jailer. No fight is left. The only open avenue appears to be the flight toward self-slaughter.

A jailer stood on the bridge looking down at the rocks below. Whose faces passed before his mind's eye? The memories of his children? The loving embrace of his wife? The destruction and darkness of an eternal beyond he was about to hurl himself into?

What hovers before you as you stand on the edge of the bridge? Tear-stained memories of the ones you have resolved to leave behind? The troubles you are hoping to see fade away? The pure, helpless self-loathing your soul feels as the world surrounds you and the devil mercilessly taunts you?

The blade was turned inward now. The steel prepared to pierce flesh. Sinful self-pity had become resolute in its action.

"Don't harm yourself!" (Acts 16:28). A strong voice reverberated through the dark halls and empty cells. Who could possibly still be left behind? A spirit calling from the underworld? An injured soul still caught in this world?

"We are all here!" (Acts 16:28). How could that be? What magic kept such hardened criminals within their prisons? The voice sounded like it came from the deepest recesses of the fortress, where the worst criminals lay.

Jumping back on to the bridge, the jailor called for lights. *Could the men really still be here?* He saw them now—the faces of the two men who had been singing moments earlier. They looked so calm, as though miracles were nothing new to them, as though they had everything in control.

The jailer had had no control left. He thought his life was over. He had stared into the face of death. The weight sunk him down to his knees. His hands still trembled. He was off of the bridge now. He still had his life. But all he could think about was the next one.

"Sirs, what must I do to be saved?" (Acts 16:29).

Whatever it was, he would do it. They now stood as the calm in midst of his storm. Maybe they had the answer.

"Believe in the Lord Jesus and you will be saved, you and your household" (Acts 16:31). And he did. His entire family did. He washed Paul and Silas' wounds, then they washed him with the powerful waters of baptism. No delay, no more darkness, no more peering into the rocks below. "He rejoiced…" Not because he saved himself, but "because he and his whole household had come to believe in God" (Acts 16:34).

Have you stood on that bridge, wondering if anyone cares enough to call out and bring you back down? I've been there, standing precariously on the railing, looking forlornly at the sharp angles below. The constant, powerful water tumbling over the rapids pulls a person in, like the hypnotizing eyes of a snake. Then, all at once, the stark reality of the precarious position shocks me back on my heels, like the snake's venomous fangs.

Don't let the devil pull you down there. The escape he shows you isn't really an escape. It isn't your only option. Please…please hear the Lord calling to you in his Word. See Jesus looking at you—not with the angry face of a tyrant—but the smiling face of your Savior. He loves you so very much. He must—after all, he gave his life for you. That life you now live, it belongs to him. He gives you family members and friends and pastors and good Christian counselors to listen to your struggles.

Your loved ones are here to hold your hand. Let them speak God's words of comfort and forgiveness to you, reminding you that you are loved, and that you have a future—when God calls you home in his time.

That future—*your* future—is heaven. The wooden bridge to that eternity is Jesus' cross. He will carry you over the deep water and the rough rocks—to the joy beyond.

In his good time…

Comfort for the Night

"Don't harm yourself… Believe in the Lord Jesus and you will be saved" (Acts 16:28,31).

CHAPTER 38

A Night on Death Row

Acts 23:11

There is an old Spanish saying: "It is impossible for you to die on the eve of your death."[1] Did you catch the confession in those words? The Spanish admit they fear of death. But they invented this quote so that they do not fear the moments before death.

It makes sense, doesn't it? Why fear the moments before your final demise. They are incapable of ending your life.

Death must have hovered heavy over Martin Luther as he spent the night in the residence of The Knights of St. John. The Holy Roman Emperor, who himself was a Spaniard named Charles V, had called Luther to a Diet in the town of Worms in 1521. The pope himself was unable to make the trip, so his representatives sat in his place. These papal legates, along with the princes and the Holy Roman Emperor, represented the most powerful thrones in Europe.

The poor monk, Martin Luther stood before them. They sat, facing him because they were not happy with him. They were irate with his writings. They wanted him to "recant" by having them destroyed.

Luther begged for more time to consider the question. He had hoped for a discussion regarding his writings—or at least a hearing. It never came. They simply commanded him to take them back. Luther's very life hung in the balance. The foundations of his faith

---

[1] Garrett M. Graff, "On September 11, Blind Luck Decided Who Lived or Died," (The Atlantic, Sept. 10, 2019). Accessed 9-11-2019 at https://www .theatlantic.com/ideas/archive/2019/09/september-11-blind-luck-decided -who-lived-or-died/597688/)

looked as though they might be squashed out. Graciously, the court gave Luther one night to think things over. He would return the next day to give his answer.

What must that night have been like for Martin Luther? Not much has been passed down to us regarding his personal thoughts and conversations. Only bits and pieces of correspondence and prayer remain.

Yet even as princes, emperors and church authorities would be sitting before him, Luther understood the real, spiritual magnitude of the situation. While he was traveling to Worms, Luther wrote to his old friend, George Spalatin: "Indeed, Christ is alive, and I shall enter Worms in spite of the gates of hell and the powers of darkness."[2]

On the night of April 17, 1521, the evening before Luther would have to stand and give his final answer before the rulers of his world, darkness must have come in many forms. There is a special German word Luther often used to describe the trials, temptations and afflictions we go through as believers. He called it *Anfechtung*. It is one of those German words that takes many English words to translate correctly.

Perhaps the tribulations brought on by the temptations of the devil that evening define the word better than any definition. Not only did physical darkness descend on Luther that night, but the powers of darkness with them. The devil knew the importance of this meeting at Worms. Luther and his stance on Scripture threatened Satan's Babylonian Captivity of the Christian Church. If he could not stop Luther with physical imprisonment or death, he would need to lead him to doubt.

The night must have been a struggle. Luther's sinful nature would have been hard at work trying to convince him to save himself and acquiesce to those more powerful. The world was already teaming up against him. And the devil must have hurled every temptation at him. *How can you be sure you are right? What good is all this if you die at the end of it?*

The Apostle Paul had similar struggles. He knew *Anfechtung* as well as Luther. His world had turned against him, too. Some of the rulers of his day vehemently stood against him and what he believed.

---

[2] E. G. Schwiebert, *Luther and His Times* (St. Louis: Concordia Publishing House, 1950), 499.

His Roman protectors could not have cared less about the religious convictions that got him in prison. And like Luther, Paul's sinful nature must have been working overtime on his thoughts as he sat in the Roman barracks.

The devil creeps into our lives at those moments. When darkness descends, the prince of darkness pushes doubts into our minds. *Why stand on your faith when it will just get you killed?* The technology of your world offers you even more opportunities to proclaim your faith. Yet the vehement objections of others can return just as quickly to you through those avenues. *Why put your beliefs out there if you are only going to get pummeled for it?*

"It is impossible for you to die on the eve of your death."

In the middle of a night of concern, worry, struggle and…well… *Anfechtung*, the Lord came to Paul with a loving encouragement. He *stood next to him* and proclaimed, "Take courage!" Was Paul's courage failing? Is your courage failing? Your Lord speaks to you with the truth of his everlasting, imperishable word. Paul could not die on the eve of his death. In fact, he would not die tomorrow either. "As you have solemnly testified about me in Jerusalem, so you must also testify in Rome" (Acts 23:11). Nothing and no one could stop him from getting to Rome. The Lord was with him.

The Lord stood by Martin Luther as he weathered those storms of doubt and fear. As he waited for the sun to rise on the morrow, he was reminded that he was not alone. While Luther waited, his friend Ulrich von Hutten wrote him a note: "Be strong and courageous. You must realize what is staked on you, what a crisis this is. You must never doubt me as long as you are constant; I will cling to you to my last breath."[3]

They were the words of a close friend and supporter. Over the ages our loving God has shared those encouragements with countless struggling saints—men on the eve of a great conquest (Josh 1:6), young kings preparing to ascend the throne (1 Chr 28:20), and cities under siege (2 Chr 32:7). These encouragements are meant for you, also.

Think of every form of *Anfechtung* you have faced. The devil will continue to hold your faith over the fire of his temptations. The

---

[3] E. G. Schwiebert, *Luther and His Times* (St. Louis: Concordia Publishing House, 1950), 828.

world around you will thrust you into tribulations of cultural pres-
sures to rip apart your faith. Your sinful nature will try so very hard
to silence the proclamation of your belief in God's Word. These are
the *Anfechtung* to which you were called at your baptism.

But remember the One who called you at your baptism. Your
Father brought you into his family. The Son purchased and won you
into this family. The Holy Spirit continues to keep and preserve you
in this family of believers by his grace and the power of his word. You
are not alone. You are *never* alone.

Martin Luther was never alone. The long night finally ended.
The next day eventually arrived. There, on their thrones, the representatives of Church and State awaited the answer of the lonely looking
monk. Would he recant? Had the weight of every form of *Anfechtung*
undermined his stalwart confession?

The question rang out again, echoing through the crowded hall.
"Will you defend these books all together, or do you wish to recant
some of what you have said?"[4]

Luther responded with a short speech. He ended with these
strong and courageous words: "Unless I can be instructed and convinced with evidence from the Holy Scriptures or with open, clear,
and distinct grounds and reasoning—and my conscience is captive
to the Word of God—then I cannot and will not recant, because it is
neither safe nor wise to act against conscience. Here I stand. I can do
no other. God help me! Amen."[5]

Your Savior, Jesus stands next to you...even in your moments
of *Anfechtung*, whispering to you what he has proclaimed to so many
other believers across time...

Comfort for the Night

"Take courage!" (Acts 23:11).

---

[4] James M. Kittelson, *Luther the Reformer* (Minneapolis: Augsburg
Publishing House, 1986), 161.

[5] Kittelson, 161.

CHAPTER 39

The Sleepless Sea

Acts 27:14-26

On the morning September 30, 2015, an audio device from the bridge of the freighter *El Faro* recorded a conversation. The captain, Michael Davidson, was discussing the weather with his Chief Mate, Steven Shultz. Neither of them knew it at the time, but this would be their final day on earth. Their last conversations on the bridge of *El Faro* are all that remain from their treacherous voyage through the Bahamas.[1]

"Red in the morning, sailors take warning. That is bright."[2] Captain Davidson's ominous words begin a nearly 500 page transcript made from that little recording box. Over the next few hours, as a tropical storm strengthens right in front of them, calm conversation slowly washes into concerned communication. The second and third mates share their concerns, suggesting a change in their route. Captain Davidson remains unmoved. "Oh. No no no. We're not gonna turn around."[3]

The morning rains form giant waves in the afternoon. A sailor can be heard asking the Third Mate, "Oh man, if you gotta divert if that hurricane veers quickly—how much time do you have to, you know, when it's set up—if you gotta duck inside?"[4] Riehm, the Third

---

[1] Audio transcript accessed on July 17, 2020, at https://www.document cloud.org/documents/3237729-El-Faro-VDR-Audio-Transcript-8510451-ver1 -0.html

[2] Transcript, 47.

[3] Transcript, 164.

[4] Transcript, 255.

Mate, was starting to feel the weight of the situation, "Well, right now, we got nowhere to go."[5]

He was right. The night wears on. Wave after wave crashes against the hull. The ship loses power. *El Faro* is drifting now, straight toward the hurricane. By 7:30 am, October 1, 2015, the sound of alarms fills the cabin. Captain Davidson has just ordered everyone overboard.

Then the ears of that little box in the corner hear one final exchange. A sailor crouches in the corner, frozen by fear, unable to move. "We gotta move. You gotta get up. You gotta snap out of it and we gotta get out," Davidson yells to him over the alarms. "Help me," the sailor pleads to his captain. He isn't hurt. He sees the hopelessness of his situation. He is facing death.

"I'm a goner!" He yells, loudly enough for the recorder to hear. Davidson firmly shouts back, "No you're not…It's time to come this way…" At that very moment the recording cuts out. It is assumed that the *El Faro* and all souls aboard slipped into the sea at that point, pushed under by the full force of a hurricane. All 33 sailors perished.

After a month-long search, covering almost 250,000 square miles a navy submersible finally found the remains of the sunken ship. They grabbed the little recording box that held inside her the audio of the crew's final hours.

Such finds always seem bittersweet. Families of the deceased, investigators, and reporters all pour over the details. This information helps answer the *how* of the tragedy. But it rarely answers the *why*. In fact, the recording might even feel like too much information. The moments before an untimely death almost seem too surreal, or even too sacred, to play before the public. We hear sailors arguing, a defiant captain, and a cowering crewman. And in the end, the most brutal truth still remains: None of this information can bring the dead back to life.

In Acts 27, we view a transcript of sorts. Luke, the writer assigned with the role of little-black-box-in-the-corner, records the frustrated cries and fearful voices of sailors aboard a ship. Hurricane-like winds drove the helpless ship along. Gales rushing off Crete, momentary

---

[5] Transcript, 255.

shelter near Cauda, the sandbars of Syrtis—nothing seemed to help the poor, battered ship.

The crew, with the Apostle Paul among them, felt just as battered. The sea had sapped their strength. They floated aimlessly, rudderless, without a single star to guide them. Eventually, hope itself seemed to have jumped overboard.

At this point, Luke records one of the most poignant phrases in the entire New Testament. The writer of a gospel book, the companion of the stalwart missionary and apostle Paul, wrote these words into the record: "Finally all hope that we would be saved was disappearing" (Acts 27:20).

We can understand heathen Roman sailors losing hope. From their perspective the god of the sea, Neptune, often stormed through their seas. We can even sympathize with the businessmen who had just dumped their valuable cargo overboard. Their livelihood might never recover. But even Paul and Luke were starting to give up hope on their physical salvation at sea.

Paul had even been here before. In his second letter to the church in Corinth, Paul wrote, "Three times I was shipwrecked. I have spent a night and a day on the open sea" (2 Cor 11:25). Worse yet were the sleepless nights he had experienced. They were such strong memories that Paul actually mentioned them *twice* in his letter (2 Cor 6:5 and 11:27).

The storms in our lives have a way of submerging us under grief and guilt. Sleepless nights usually follow. Adrift, clutching the floating boards of a once-steady ship, you now feel alone. Your sins, your struggles seem as vast as the ocean; as powerful as a hurricane. When faith starts to sink and the ship breaks apart, a lonely death seems like the only possible end. The little black box sitting in the corner of your mind forms a transcript that might sound like the final words of that sailor aboard the El Faro. "Help me...I'm a goner!"

Who could ever sleep at such a time?

Jesus could. Jesus *did*. Once again playing the role of little-black-box, Luke writes about another sailing disaster. He wasn't on the boat this time, but Jesus and his disciples were. "A powerful windstorm came down on the lake, the boat was filling up with water, and they were in danger" (Luke 8:23).

But Jesus was still asleep. He wasn't acting asleep or pretending to be calm. He really was calm. The storm battered their boat. Waves washed over his fisherman disciples. And there in the eye of the storm, the serene Savior slept.

Then Luke's transcript picks up what sounds like the final words aboard the boat: "Master, master, we're going to die!" (Luke 8:24). The shouts echoed like a last resort. For those disciples it likely was.

Calmly, the master and commander of the seas and the waves and the wind and the ship and the sailors stood up. Here another little-black-box, the Gospel of Mark, records the words the Savior declared into the storm: "Peace. Be still" (Mark 4:39). And all at once there was peace. Everything became still.

So, it would be for Luke and Paul aboard their ship, too. The shipwreck was coming. A hazardous float to a nearby island was still on the horizon. But in the depths of his hopelessness, when the black night looked as though it would consume them all, an angel of the Lord came aboard and stood beside Paul. "Do not be afraid, Paul. You must stand before Caesar" (Acts 27:24). And Paul would not be the only survivor. "Surely God has graciously given you all those who are sailing with you" (Acts 27:24).

God sees you, drifting through the treacherous waters of your everyday life. He knows your sorrows. He feels your hurt. He hears your every sigh, even the ones a little-black-box cannot make out. And he knows all of this because he is right there with you, standing aboard your boat. You are not sailing alone. Your Lord, the one who calmed the storm on Galilee, the one who saved Paul and Luke on their voyage to Rome, the one who weathered the storm of your every sin on the cross stands with you. His words still echo across the waters of time - words not just for the wind and the waves, but for you...

Comfort for the Night

"Peace. Be still" (Mark 4:39).

Chapter 40

Darkness Obliterated

Revelation 22:3-5

"Graciously keep me this night." Those nighttime words have ascended to the Lord from desert sands, snowy mountain tops and vast oceans. Across thousands of years, verbalized in countless languages, the hearts of troubled men and women have poured forth those pleas. Adam must have thought them as he stepped across the cursed ground after that fateful day he fell into sin. Haunted kings spoke them with tearstained faces. Suffering servants petitioned the Lord as they endured nights that seemed to last forever. Fathers wept over the graves of their children, wondering if the agony they felt in their bones would ever fade away.

It has been a long walk for us through these nights, too. The moon has reflected light over our nighttime worries. Guilt has stalked us. The devil has tried to separate us from our Good Shepherd while the evening grows ever darker.

Martin Luther's evening prayer has accompanied us through it all. Perhaps we appreciate those words even more now that we find ourselves at the end. After all, Luther knew what he was talking about. He had watched helplessly as his beloved daughter passed away from this life. He struggled to trust in his Lord when the world put him on the defense for his faith. He intimately felt how black the nights of this sinful world could become.

I think that is why Luther was a master of prayer. Like a soldier in battle, Luther had faced the enemy. His feet knew how hot the fire of temptation could get. His prayer life illustrated how fierce the good fight had become for him.

And in this beautiful prayer life, Martin Luther shares a most practical wisdom. He approaches his Lord not by firing off one selfish request after another. No, in the darkest of nights, Luther approaches his Lord with thanksgiving. Because there are always so many reasons for a believer to give his Father thanks.

"I thank you my heavenly Father."

Shall we number the ways God provides for us? Life and breath certainly lead us to give thanks. Family and friends cannot be forgotten. Food and health need to be recounted from a thankful heart as well. But Luther gets right to the heart of it all - the Source of everything good.

"Through Jesus Christ your dear Son."

In a particularly pointed hymn, Luther once intimated just how much we owe our Savior Jesus:

"If God had not been on our side And had not come to aid us,

Our foes with all their pow'r and pride Would surely have dismayed us."[1]

The understanding, of course, is that God is on our side. We need look no further than today to see just how much our Lord loves us.

"You have graciously kept me this day."

Distractions, worries, busy schedules probably kept us from fully seeing the intricacies of God's love for us during this day. It is so easy to take God's protection and providence for granted! Martin Luther makes us enunciate at least once during the day that God has indeed "kept" us in his almighty, loving hands.

In fact, we have forgotten God's goodness on a day to day basis. Again this day we tried to take control. We thought we needed to solve our own problems. We wondered if God really cared enough to help. Our minds conjured up sinful thoughts. Our mouths poured out poisonous words. Our actions broke commandments left and right. Luther wants us to be honest about that, too.

"Forgive me all my sins."

Then comes the petition we have carried with us. In light of Jesus' boundless love for us, you can approach your Father in heaven

---

[1] Wisconsin Evangelical Lutheran Synod, *Christian Worship* (Milwaukee: Northwestern Publishing House, 1993), 202.

with a request—a most important request! As the sun sets, as the distractions dissipate, as your mind wanders, as the blackness of guilt and doubt creep into your heart, you get to pray the words of a helpless child to his father.

"Graciously keep me this night."

In the end, our lives, our days, our nights all belong to him anyway. We just need to verbalize that truth in order to remember it all over again. This is the time to "be still" and know that our Father in heaven "is God" (Ps 46:10).

"Into your hands I commend my body and soul and all things."

The reminder has jumped from these pages again and again: You are not alone. You are *never* alone. Only one man was ever truly alone on this earth. He willingly walked to the loneliest place of all. He allowed the small, sinful hands of this world to bind him to your cross. His Father turned away from him there, abandoning him to hell. And he endured all of it so that you never will. In fact, he protects you from the very one for whom that hell was originally made.

"Let your holy angel be with me that the wicked foe may have no power over me."

There Jesus stood. Evening was falling. The roads that had echoed with the noise of that busy Palm Sunday now rested quietly. The Lord of all, the Author of life, the Orchestrator of time and space had allowed himself a few moments alone before the temple.

It still amazes me that Jesus took time to take it all in. He looked out across the stones that had witnessed faithful worship and cries of defiance. He saw the altar of sacrifice upon which the blood of countless animals had poured out in his direction. He focused on the curtain inside that in just a few short days would no longer be needed.

Every intricate detail, each action pointed to him. And for just one quiet moment, the Lord could look backward and forward at the same time. The Prophet had come to finish his perfect sermon. The High Priest was about to sacrifice himself. The King of kings would set aside his heavenly throne to set up a throne in your heart.

The night would come. Jesus, the Word once spoken to create all light, the Light of the world, would take the darkness of eternal death upon himself. He accomplished it all for *you*.

This dark, sometimes horrific world is not your home. Tonight will end. Really, it will. And joy will return. Here in this sin-filled world that joy will be muted. It will come and go. But your eternal joy is coming. It couldn't be more different from what you have been living through here on earth. The Apostle John saw it from a distance. He wrote down what he saw. But listen to how he describes your heaven: "I did not see a temple in the city, because the Lord God Almighty and the Lamb are its temple. The city does not need the sun or the moon to shine on it, because the glory of God has given it light, and the Lamb is its lamp" (Rev 22:22-23).

No need for a temple. Not one single streetlight or lightbulb. And did you catch why? "There is no day when its gates will be shut, for there will be no night in that place" (Rev 22:25). What will that be like? You don't know yet, but you will. Look to that sure and certain light of heaven when the blackness of this world tries to pull you down. You have a hope. You have a future. And it is all through your Savior, your Light. That's why we end our prayer with the same word Luther did...

"Amen."

"The God who said, 'Light will shine out of darkness,' is the same one who made light shine in our hearts" (2 Cor 4:6). And he does shine in you, even in the moments when you don't feel it. And when the devil throws your head down to distract you from your light-filled eternity, then pray. Pray to your Lord, you Light. Pray those words that sounded forth from struggling souls across deserts and mountains and oceans. Cast your guilt and your agony upon the Lord who came to take it all away. "Graciously keep me this night."

No need to fear, fellow believer. Jesus is your strength, your salvation, your all in all—tonight and always...

Comfort for the Night

"Do not be afraid. I am the First and the Last—the Living One. I was dead and, see, I am alive forever and ever!" (Rev 1:17).